P9-CRS-976

GO
Bravely

"In a world that often offers young women choices that steal joy and are based in fear, *Go Bravely* is a book that counteracts this culture of mediocrity and challenges young women to embrace a life of adventure and holy greatness. When wondering how to act bravely in life, Emily Wilson Hussem leaves readers with practical tools that give strength and bravery in facing their own challenges. *Go Bravely* is the most honest, practical, and encouraging book a young woman could read (and should read) today."

Leah Darrow
International speaker and author of *The Other Side of Beauty*

"*Go Bravely* helps young women to navigate the often turbulent waters of our society. With ease and clarity, *Go Bravely* is able to confirm each woman in her identity of being a daughter of God while at the same time giving the support to live out this identity in a world that desperately needs the witness of joyful, Catholic femininity."

Rev. Joseph-Anthony Kress, O.P.
Chaplain at the University of Virginia

"*Go Bravely* is a beautiful adventure into the heart of what it means to live as a vibrant and joyful young woman. Through her honesty, wisdom, and wit, Emily invites the reader into a deeper encounter with Jesus and into what really matters in life. I highly recommend it!"

Sr. Miriam James Heidland, S.O.L.T.
Author of *Loved as I Am*

"With authenticity and humility, Emily Wilson Hussem reminds us that we are never alone in our struggles. It's good to be told that you are a beloved daughter of God; it's even better to be shown how to live out that reality. Emily does this in the spirit of friendship, grasping hold of your hand, charting a new path, and offering encouragement each step of the way. While sharing the vision of where God wants you to be, *Go Bravely* reminds you over and over again that you are and will always be loved. If you long to pursue God with your whole heart, this book will help you move forward on that journey."

Lisa Brenninkmeyer
Author, speaker, and founder of Walking with Purpose

"*Go Bravely* is a must-have book for young women. This down-to-earth and practical book is almost as good as having a cup of coffee with Emily herself! Through her personal stories, humor, and wisdom, you feel like she is walking with you and cheering you on so that you can be empowered to be the woman God created you to be."

Jackie Francois-Angel
Recording artist and speaker

"In *Go Bravely*, Emily Wilson Hussem offers practical—and joyful—strategies for living as a Christian woman in today's culture. Her inspirational witness and down-to-earth advice make this book a must-read for any young women seeking to illuminate the world with the witness of their lives."

Jason Evert
Author, speaker, and founder of the Chastity Project

GO
Bravely

BECOMING THE
WOMAN YOU WERE
CREATED TO BE

EMILY WILSON HUSSEM

Ave Maria Press AVE Notre Dame, Indiana

Unless otherwise stated, scripture quotations are from *New Revised Standard Version Bible*, copyright © 1989 National Council of the Churches of Christ in the United States of America. Used by permission. All rights reserved.

© 2018 by Emily Wilson Hussem

All rights reserved. No part of this book may be used or reproduced in any manner whatsoever, except in the case of reprints in the context of reviews, without written permission from Ave Maria Press®, Inc., P.O. Box 428, Notre Dame, IN 46556, 1-800-282-1865.

Founded in 1865, Ave Maria Press is a ministry of the United States Province of Holy Cross.

www.avemariapress.com

Paperback: ISBN-13 978-1-59471-825-0

E-book: ISBN-13 978-1-59471-826-7

Cover images © Adobe Stock.

Cover and text design by Brianna Dombo.

Printed and bound in the United States of America.

Library of Congress Cataloging-in-Publication Data is available.

For my mom,

who brilliantly, beautifully, and selflessly
taught me what it means to be a brave,
bold woman of faith.

Contents

Introduction

A round, brilliant-cut diamond reflects the most light of all the cuts of diamonds in the world. The formula for the brilliant cut, also known as the Tolkowsky cut, is designed so that the diamond reflects up to 92 percent of the light that shines into its dozens of facets. This incredible and breathtaking reflection of light makes the round, brilliant cut a very popular choice for men when they are seeking out the perfect engagement ring.

Like a brilliant-cut diamond, our lives as young women of faith have dozens of facets. We are expected to juggle school, family, relationships, faith, activities, drama, our appearance, social life, friendships, community, and more. Not only are we expected to juggle these things, but we are expected to juggle them all well, even though we are never given an instruction manual on how to execute this! It is not easy! In the center of the many aspects of life as a happy, healthy, and virtuous young woman lies our identity in Christ, our identity as daughters of God. We are to keep this at the center of all that we do, but this is no simple endeavor. It is, however, a worthwhile one. When we are consistently aware of the core of who we are—daughters of the almighty God—we let God's love flow into every aspect of our lives, and we begin to reflect *his* light. We begin to let his radiant love shine through the darkness of our broken world. We become the women he created us to be, and through this, we begin to look much like a brilliant, illuminated diamond.

It is impossible to cover every facet of womanhood in any forty-five-minute talk I present to a group of women. There are so many things to cover in talking about womanhood in its entirety. So, I have compiled many of the topics that are important for women to talk about in this book. I want to open up conversations among women about how we can find balance in our lives and how we can make decisions that reflect our dignity and worth, as well as strengthen us to live out our femininity in the way God designed us to. I want to create actionable points that we can incorporate into our daily lives, as I also share my own journey as a young woman of faith to encourage, inspire, and help you on your journey. I want to help you believe in yourself more. I want to help you recognize that you are braver and stronger than you probably think you are. You are my sister in Christ, and I want you to feel me cheering you on as we unpack these facets of womanhood.

The goal of this book is not to tell you how to live, and I do not and never will promise to have all the answers to all of life's questions, but I did survive high school and college trying my very best to pursue virtue and live my life as a young woman of faith and joy, and I can speak to that. I can offer you my witness. I can share my own experience that magnifying God in my choices, in the way I treat others, and in the way I treat myself is tremendously difficult but altogether possible for me and for you. Many of the things in this book are very challenging to live out; if it was easy to live virtue wholeheartedly, everyone would be doing it. Why? Because a life of virtue and of choosing to follow Christ is a gateway to living as a woman who embodies peace and joy—and our world certainly needs more peaceful, joyful, and radiant women.

I have found that bravery is the main component required for living as a young woman of faith in our world today. If you want to live virtue and proclaim a wholehearted faith in your words and actions, you have to be bold. You have to be brave. It takes courage to uphold a high set of values, to share your love for God in a world in which faith is extremely unpopular, and to go against the flow. It takes courage to let go of worrying about what other people may think or say about you and to follow the path that God lights before you. It is not popular to love Jesus and to follow him with your whole heart. It is not easy to choose faith continually, and it is challenging to live the bravery that our faith requires of us, but I have some ideas on how we can make it easier on ourselves.

My hope is that as you read this book, you will feel as though you and I are sitting together at a coffee shop, having long, wonderful conversations about the joys and struggles of womanhood. It would be a delight for me to be able to have coffee with you because I am a woman with struggles and questions just like you, trying to juggle everything well and to love Jesus well at the same time. We are in this together. I want to invite you on this journey with me, and I pray that you will have an open heart to what God wants to reveal to you and stir up in your heart through these pages. May you and I both have an openness to the ways he wants us to reflect his light and his love—and go bravely forward in our world, living as the radiant, courageous women God so carefully and lovingly created us to be.

ONE

Go Bravely

Throughout the first few years of high school, I didn't know what I wanted to "do" with my life. There were endless possibilities of careers to choose from, and I didn't know which one I was most passionate about. I signed up for an elective video-production class on a whim my senior year, thinking it would be fun. I had no idea that class would change the course of my life forever.

Through this class and the passion of my wonderful teachers, Mr. and Mrs. Gillen, I became very drawn to the field of journalism, video, and media. I began to have lofty dreams of becoming a sports reporter for ESPN after spending many memorable Sundays and Monday nights watching football with my dad while growing up. I began to research colleges with prestigious journalism schools, and one school that kept coming up in my research was Arizona State University in Tempe, Arizona. ASU boasted the best journalism school on the West Coast and was very affordable compared to most of the other schools on my list, so I went on a fun visit in the spring with my dad and felt it was a great fit for me. I applied, was accepted, and after having attended small private schools my entire life, I set out for ASU, a place where young people of faith were an extreme minority. It was unconventional, and somewhat confusing to people, that I chose to attend a large public school, well known for its party scene, as a young woman who loved God and wanted to follow him.

Throughout high school, I chose to live my faith and dedicated myself to making good choices and trying to follow Christ in every aspect of my life. Attending Arizona State, however, required a bravery that I had not anticipated in continuing on this path. Stepping onto my college campus was a massive shift from everything that I was accustomed to in the small, intimate communities I had grown up in. Faith life was not prevalent at all, but in the beginning of my freshman year, I found a chapel on my campus. It was an interfaith chapel located in the center of campus, called the Danforth Chapel, and it was conveniently located within a two-minute walk from my dorm. Every day a priest from the Newman Center would come to celebrate a Catholic Mass in this chapel at 11:40 a.m., and this fit in my schedule, so I tried to attend every day, as it was something my mother raised me to love by taking me to church every day with her as a child. The most difficult part of getting to this Mass on campus, however, had nothing to do with scheduling difficulties: *The biggest challenge was mustering up the bravery to walk through the door of the chapel when I knew everyone around could see me going in to pray.*

There were days when I felt utterly embarrassed to be living my faith and to be seen walking through those doors to a Mass that was attended by a maximum of twelve people on a crowded day. As a young woman who was active in youth group in high school, I couldn't believe the difficulty of this one small act on some days. Each time I put my hand on the doorknob and felt self-conscious about going in to pray, I began to say a simple prayer quietly but out loud: "Jesus, help me to be brave." I did it again and again—every day for months—and it was through the act of opening this door every day that I learned a lesson that I tucked away in my heart for the rest of my life: *Sometimes even the smallest acts of living out faith require great bravery.*

Bravery is not the absence of fear but the ability to conquer our fears and choose to do the right thing. To be a brave woman of faith is to make decisions that bring us closer to God, even though these decisions can often be difficult or uncomfortable. If you've ever stood in a river or an ocean with a strong current, you know how difficult it is to move your legs to walk against that current. That feeling is synonymous with the challenge of living life as a young woman of faith at a large university. I felt the tension of walking against the current on most days, and it would have been easy to give up and let myself be picked up by the current of what was accepted and "normal." I would not have stood out for being the "good girl." I would have blended into the crowd along with everyone else. Nobody would have asked me questions about why I stayed home on the weekends rather than going out to parties or why I put in all the effort to bike to church on Sundays. But somehow—with the help of a mighty God who walked beside me through it all—I kept living bravery.

The bravery that I was called to live beyond opening that chapel door was the bravery to live a life that was radically different from what my college campus was advocating as normal and accepted. I was surrounded by my peers, the majority of whom were often drunk, high, or sleeping around on many nights. I was living my faith, maintaining my core values, trying to make good choices, and doing everything I could to stay close to God. I couldn't have been living a more radically different life than a majority of the people around me, and the more I lived a completely different life, the more difficult it was to be brave, because this bravery made way for moments, days, and weeks of painful loneliness. I was trying to be brave, but I felt like an outcast. People made sure that I knew I was a misfit among my peers, and I realized very quickly that feelings of loneliness can very easily convince anyone that being brave isn't worth the trouble.

Those feelings of loneliness made every attempt to convince me that it's not worth it to be brave in this world, that it's not worth it to live differently, that it would be easier to give up on trying to walk against the current and instead just go with the flow. My loneliness was very loud in its attempts to get me to quit. So in order to combat these feelings of loneliness and of being an outcast, I derived my strength from my relationship with God. In all the difficulty of being courageous, I continually asked God for the strength to do it. I visited the chapel frequently to pray. I persisted in asking him to help me stay strong in going against the flow with that simple little prayer, "Jesus, help me to be brave." I continually asked him to walk with me, to give me the strength to open the door to the chapel, to help me decline friendly invitations to places or events that would lead me away from him. He did.

As I have done my best to live my faith, I have come to see that bravery inspires bravery. Have you ever been inspired by the bravery of another woman you know? I have multiple women in my life who have become my role models because of the way they bravely live their lives and their faith. Everyone has a different definition of the term "role model," but I believe that a role model is someone who declares to others simply by their actions: "If I can do it, you can, too." You can be a role model to the women around you by your bravery. Perhaps your gut reaction to that thought is to say, "No way." Yes, way. This requires stepping out of the huddle, out of the groups of people in social circles who are terrified to live in a way that may make them look different or foolish to their peers. Yes, it can be very difficult at times, but you have all the bravery needed to live out your faith and make good choices for yourself because the God, the author of all strength and bravery, is fighting for you, defending you, and *with* you in every moment (see Exodus 14:14).

You will have moments and seasons when you feel very different from others if you are living your faith in this millennium—there is no way around that. You may continually feel as though you are walking against a strong current, perpetually going against the flow of the world. But you will be called to push through in the moments, seasons, and even years when you feel like an outcast in a world where you do not belong. If you choose to live a life as a strong, faithful, loving, self-respecting woman, you can be a role model to the women around you to show them that it is possible to live such a life, that it is beautiful to live such a life, that it is truly and deeply fulfilling to live such a life. You can inspire the women around you to think quietly in their hearts, most especially in the moments of great difficulty: *If she can do it, I can, too.*

There will be small moments and massive moments in which you will be called by your faith to be brave. Use that prayer, again and again, as many times as you need to, in the moments when you feel like quitting because something or someone is trying to convince you it's too hard: "Jesus, help me to be brave."

May Jesus help us, always and in everything, to live a bravery derived from his heart and his strength. I pray he helps each of us to persevere, and to always choose the path that will outwardly reflect his light and his love.

. . . .

TAKE ACTION

Consider what the word "brave" means to you.
Reflect on these questions:

- What does it mean to be brave?
- Do you feel that you are a brave person?

TWO

Remember Who You Are

Women are excellent at possessing many titles. We are naturally inclined to be good at multitasking (i.e., our ability to measure out all the ingredients for baking delicious brownies while carrying on a deep conversation on the phone or being able to iron a dress while catching up on our favorite TV show). Our tendency to get involved in many activities, which is often compounded by extreme pressure, piles on the titles. Perhaps you hold the title of sister, student, or leader. Perhaps you're an aunt, a vice president, a volleyball player, a friend, a missionary, a mentor, a confidante, a cook, or a teacher. What are some of the titles you possess? The titles we live out in our activities or service of others are beautiful things, but often we pour so much of ourselves into living out these titles that it becomes almost natural to make them our identity. If someone asks me, "Who are you?"

I am very inclined to tell them my name and some of the titles I hold in my life, such as wife, speaker, and singer.

You may hold a hundred different titles like the ones I have mentioned, but none of those titles will ever stand as your truest and deepest identity. You are not first a student, or fashion designer, or blogger. You are, first and above all, a daughter.

You are a daughter of God. "See what love the Father has given us, that we should be called children of God" (1 John 3:1a).

By the grace of Baptism, we become children of God. And "daughter of God" is not just another title to add to the list of ones you already have. Daughter of God is *who you are.*

There is an incalculable depth to this reality and identity, but perhaps it has become cliché for you. You may have heard it countless times, on retreats or in church, over and over again. I grew tired of hearing that I am a "princess," a daughter of the King, because it was told to me so often and in such a cheesy way that it didn't resonate in my bones in the way that this reality is supposed to. I was once told on a retreat that I'm a princess and should *wave my wand high* (like Glinda the good witch, or something). No, thanks. But after years of searching and discovering more about who I am as a woman, I have come to recognize one truth over and over again about my identity as daughter of God. I have a Father in heaven who created me, who loves me with a relentless kind of love that would make my heart explode if I actually understood it, and who is always with me (see Isaiah 41:10). This is an unchanging reality of which I can only understand an infinitesimal fraction, but it is the truth of who I am, and the truth of who you are. This is the most spectacular thing about you. It is the most magnificent declaration that has ever been made over your life.

When we consciously live with this truth resonating in our hearts, it changes everything.

The truth of this identity changes everything because it means that you are and always will be loved. There is not a moment in your life during which you will not be loved.

This truth is jam-packed with breathtaking beauty, but it is also chock-full of challenges. This identity changes everything because it requires an intentional way of life. As daughters of God, we do not live for ourselves; we live for a greater purpose— to bring glory to God the Father. But this intentionality that is asked of us poses a great challenge to us because it should affect every aspect of our lives in a positive and profound way.

Living out your identity as daughter of God is unconventional, and it calls you to hard things. It does not require sinless perfection from you—but it does call you to pursue God with your whole heart. It asks that you lead a life that looks different than the lives many other women are leading around you. It asks you to stand out, to be different, to walk and live in courage and fortitude. It calls you to rise above the life that our culture is proclaiming is "normal."

As women of faith, we can't be "normal." If we take a brief moment to look at what is considered "normal" in our world today, it is a very good thing that we are called to live differently.

Life, however, is a very full and sometimes confusing and tumultuous thing. Sometimes the reality of who we are falls to the wayside, and we forget our identity as daughters or we choose not to live it. When we make decisions that do not bring glory to God, when we do not make good choices for ourselves, when we allow ourselves to be influenced by the message of the world and our decisions to be swayed by our desire to fit in, we are not living out our true identity. We don't live from this place of our true identity when we fall into patterns of sin, when we tear ourselves down, when we fail to connect with God on a regular basis. When it really comes down to it, I have found one thing to be true over and over again: *It is so much easier to forget our identity as daughter than it is to live it.*

If it feels hard to give your identity as daughter of God permission to change every aspect of your life, that is a good thing. It's not supposed to be easy. Following Jesus is not a lifestyle for the faint of heart; Jesus said over and over again in the gospels that following him would not be easy but that it is the road to true and lasting fulfillment. In Luke 9:23 (NIV), he tells his disciples, "Whoever wants to be my disciple must deny themselves and take up their cross daily and follow me."

One of the most beautiful aspects of following Jesus is that we can't do whatever we want whenever we feel like it. Instead, we are led closer to him when we deny ourselves those things that would be easy to do but we know are not good for us. When we deny ourselves, when we reject the temptation to turn away from God and go our own way rather than the way we know God calls us to, we move ever closer to Christ. And it is when we are close to Christ that we find ourselves living the life he created us for—lives filled with kindness, peace, joy, and an overflowing willingness and desire to nurture the world with the kind of selfless love Christ taught us to give. Our hearts look the way he created them to when we stand in his light; his radiant love shines into them and reflects directly out of them to make beautiful things.

As daughters of God we must live differently. But it is also important to remember that this identity is not always about action. It also gives us permission to rest.

The titles the world gives us—student, singer, scientist, president, chef—do require action, either active or passive. That may include the active action of doing schoolwork or the passive action of listening to someone else's troubles. These titles require that you do something. But your identity as daughter doesn't always require doing; sometimes it only requires that you sit still and allow yourself to be loved. There is no action necessary to earn the love of God.

So often we feel as though we have to *do* something for Christ to look on us with love. We are conditioned so heavily to believe that nearly everything in life has to be earned that we begin to believe it about the love and goodness of God. However, Christ loves you *because you are.* All you have to do in order for him to love you is exist. You can bask in his presence and rest and receive. You can stand before him, overwhelmed by all the titles you are trying to juggle, neck-deep in the stresses of life, and find that you are loved intimately and that you can find peace in this kind of love.

The women in scripture were in all kinds of messy situations—and they didn't have to be in any certain place or do any certain thing for Jesus to look on them with love. Whether that was the woman caught in adultery (see John 8:1–11), the sinful woman (see Luke 7:36–50), or the woman at the well (see John 4:1–30), they only had to stand before Jesus to find true love. They only had to gaze into the eyes of Christ to know that they had finally found rest.

In his encyclical *Mulieris Dignitatem*, Pope John Paul II states that woman "cannot find herself except through a sincere gift of self. In the spirit of Christ, in fact, women can discover the entire meaning of their femininity and thus be disposed to making a 'sincere gift of self' to others, thereby finding themselves." Pope John Paul II proclaimed in this encyclical that we as women have a natural inclination to give of ourselves to others—and that it is through giving of ourselves in selfless and nurturing love that we can discover who we are. As women, we possess that natural inclination to take care, to nurture, and to give of ourselves to others.

It is likely that you either have been or will be called to give of yourself to a world in desperate need of love. You will be called to a vocation that will require you to dig in and love like Christ loved on the Cross, and there may be moments when this gift of giving yourself to others and living out all your titles will cause you to forget who you are underneath all the giving. In the midst of all the giving you will do in your life, in the midst of pouring out your feminine and selfless love into the world and into all the people God places in your path, you will always have your identity as daughter. And if you give this identity permission, it will continue to change everything.

The truth that we are daughters of God, when believed, makes us unstoppable. Soak in it. Marinate like a chicken in it. Ask God to help you believe it. It is only when we believe it that we can go forward with our heads held high, ready to take on the challenges that faith calls us to, and the beautiful plan that God wants to unfold continually before each of us.

Remember who you are. And always remember that daughters of God are not weak—they are strong, they are brave, and they shine.

. . . .

TAKE ACTION

Is there an area in your life where you are acting from a place that is not reflective of your identity as daughter? Consider how you can change those actions or patterns of behavior that don't reflect your truest identity. Are you juggling too many titles and forgetting who you are? Consider your schedule and how you can rearrange it or make some changes to fit in time to rest in the presence of God.

THREE

Be Kind to Other Women

A few years ago I was at an event, and a wonderful friend of mine who is also a speaker and musician walked into the room. I heard a woman mutter quietly and jokingly to her friend as this woman walked into the same room as me: "Oooohhh . . . competition!"

I wanted to waltz over to this woman and ask her the one question I want to pose to you: When on earth did womanhood become a competition?

About a year after our wedding, my husband, Daniël, and I traveled to Hawaii for our honeymoon. It was as fabulously relaxing and romantic as I dreamed my honeymoon would be, and we spent most of our time on the islands snorkeling. Snorkeling on the Hawaiian Islands is one of the most breathtaking things I have ever experienced because of the stunning array of fish that you are able to see. The experience is like watching artwork come alive. The fish were painted with colors I had never seen before, the most breathtaking electric blues and hot pinks, with patterns and designs on their bodies that no human could recreate in an artistic rendering. There were fish of all shapes and sizes, and the longer we snorkeled, the more fish I saw, and the more I wanted to shout with delight at God's dazzling, breath-taking artistry.

As I floated through the water and soaked in the beauty, I was overcome with the realization that these fish were so much like every woman God ever created—completely beautiful and unique. As I watched them swimming around and foraging for food, I felt a tangible sense that each of these fish was content to rest in its own resplendent individuality. They weren't jealous of each other (perhaps fish don't have a capacity for jealousy—because, well, they're fish—but I imagined this anyway), and there was an incredible tranquility to their activity. As I swam about face down with my foggy goggles suctioned tightly to my head, resting on a purple noodle, I thought to myself, *Imagine if every woman in the world felt free to rest in her brilliant individuality and stunning and unique design like a Hawaiian fish does.*

I continued to ponder this as I made my way back onto the boat. When we step back to think about it, it is not often that we are truly able to rest in the reality that each of us was individually handcrafted by God, uniquely in his image (see Genesis 1:27). So often we struggle to remember this and begin to think, *Every woman around me is far more beautiful, talented, and amazing than I am.* And do you know how this inability to celebrate our individual gifts and beauty affects us? It causes us to treat womanhood like a competition and to strive unnecessarily to be "better" than other women. It propels us to compete and to view other women as runners next to us in a race rather than as our sisters and our friends. We begin to live as though our life is a beauty pageant, as though we have to look better or have a better body or perform better than the woman standing next to us. So we begin to do everything in our power to come out on top, as we continually look left and right to ensure that we are in a position of power over other women. We want to make sure we are getting better grades, more dates, or cuter boyfriends or that we have more followers or more people paying attention to us and affirming us on every level. We strive and struggle and compete—but striving and struggling and competing is not what we were made for.

There are many situations in which competition propels people to become better; the Olympics are a terrific example of this. People push themselves very hard to prepare for the Olympics and strive to win a medal, to stand on that podium under the lights and hear their country's anthem playing loudly for all in attendance. At that moment, their spirit is uplifted because their dedication has caused them to be recognized as the best in their sport. They have worked very hard to come out on top, and when they do, it is a paramount moment. Competition makes athletes better athletes.

Competition does not, however, make women better women. It doesn't uplift us in any way; it always does the opposite. It burdens us and brings us down. It stifles our gifts and our talents.

It doesn't allow us to live joyfully as the women God created us to be.

Treating womanhood as a competition burdens us, and it can also cause us to act out. This unhealthy spirit of competition is a major root cause of why we as women can be very unkind to one another. The only reason any woman ever utters a mean comment to or about another woman is that she does not feel good about herself and wants to bring the other woman down with her. That is what we as women do; we compare ourselves with the women around us and often end up feeling as though we don't measure up, which causes insecurity in our hearts, and that insecurity drives us to tear down other women through unkind thoughts, words, and actions. It is a simple formula:

Comparison → Insecurity → Demeaning Others

I have lived out this little formula more times than I can count, and it is not something I am proud of. There was one particular season of my life when I found myself tearing other women down more often than usual. I was quick to judge other women in my heart, whether it was about their actions or their clothes or their talents. I constantly spoke negatively about other women and had an incessant flow of judgmental thoughts, to the point where I had to take a good look inside myself to see why I was acting and thinking this way. I quickly found that *insecurity*, the word in the center of this formula, was playing a very big part in the moments when I was being unkind to other women, either out loud or in my head.

I often struggle greatly with my own insecurity. I have struggled for many years with deep insecurities about who I am and the way others perceive me. I will be sharing more about that later on in our journey here together, but as I have grown and changed and worked to root out my insecurities, I have come to learn that insecurity, at its root, stems from a lack of belief in *who I am*. If I am living from the place where I remember my identity as daughter of God, aware of the truth that I was handcrafted by the divine Creator—created with the utmost care and attention with distinct gifts and abilities—then there is no need for me to be insecure. There is no need to lack confidence in who I am. But too often I forget this, and in my head I begin to compete with other women and feel as though I will never measure up to how beautiful and funny and smart and incredible they are. And it causes me to tear them down, all in a feeble and pathetic attempt to feel better about myself. And it *never* works. I never feel better. I always feel worse. No woman has ever been made happier by being uncharitable or speaking unkind words about another woman, whether to her face or behind her back.

When I was letting insecurity dominate my heart, I was never found celebrating other women. I was blaring the trumpet of my insecurity by competing and striving and putting my jealousy on display. Nobody wants to be around the woman who is constantly speaking poorly of other women all the time. Beyond that, as jealousy cluttered my heart, I realized how much it was clouding my vision. It was preventing me from seeing other women as human, as my sisters, rather than competitors. It was preventing me from engaging in true sisterhood. Sisterhood is a very powerful bond, but we fracture the bond when we project jealousy rather than kindness, when we resort to gossip and spreading rumors about other women rather than stepping back to remember, "We are on the same team. She has insecurities, burdens, and troubles just like I do. She has a story I do not know. I have not walked in her shoes. I cannot judge her. If God had wanted me to have the same gifts and talents she has, he would have given them to me. I am called to celebrate who she is and who she was created to be."

When we step back to remember the uniqueness that God instilled within each of us, it should only leave room in our souls for celebration—celebration of ourselves and of others. When we cultivate confidence within ourselves, a holy confidence that comes from knowing who we are, we are able to celebrate other women. We are able to share genuinely in their joys and accomplishments, and take part in true sisterhood.

God looks on you with love, and you are called to reflect that love into the heart of every woman you encounter throughout your life. Just like those fish, there are brilliant and breathtaking colors in your heart that the world needs to see. Perhaps it's a new shade of turquoise or the most electric neon green that anyone has ever encountered. You will never be able to share those colors with the world if you are busy being jealous of the pretty colors, gifts, and abilities God gave other women. Rest in your unique beauty and abilities, and you will find your spirit strengthened and uplifted. Women who know who they are walk side by side with other women, proclaiming by the way they speak to them and about them the truth that will remain forever: As women, we are and will always be on this journey together.

. . . .

TAKE ACTION

Think of a woman in your life whom you have struggled to see as a sister in Christ rather than as your competition. Pray for her throughout this week. Ask God to bless her and to help you celebrate her in your thoughts, words, or actions.

FOUR

Depend on Him

As women, we love to plan things. Whether it is parties, events, gatherings, celebration lunches, or manicure appointments—you name a fun thing, and we can make a whole event out of it. There are few things I love more than a girls' day out with my mom, aunt, and sisters to get lunch together and sit in massage chairs while we chat and get our nails done. I am, however, not much of an organized planner in most facets of my life. But the one thing I was always good at planning was the timeline of my life: "I'll meet my future husband by twenty-four, we'll be married by twenty-seven, and I'll have at least one baby by thirty."

Sound familiar? We love to map out our lives with excitement and anticipation. Sometimes, though, too much planning can cause us trouble. We map things out with so much eagerness and expectation that we may begin to believe that we are in control of everything. We want to plan the "party" that is our lives and ensure that it is filled with brightly colored streamers and piñatas and happiness all along the way. We may begin to think that we are responsible for making sure that our timelines go according to plan so that life turns out exactly as we hope it will. We may even begin to depend entirely on ourselves and our carefully curated plans. This dependence upon ourselves, on *our* plans and on *our* ability to control everything, never ends well— it often just ends in heartache, disappointment, and confusion.

When we try to control our own lives, timelines, and circumstances, it creates tension and anxiety in our hearts. Control of these things is simply an illusion. Controlling all the circumstances of our lives is and will always be entirely impossible. When you think about people who can be described as controlling, would you also typically describe them as peaceful? Not usually. Why? Because attempting to control things creates tension. There is no surrender. There is no trust. There is no dependence. There is only gripping tightly and grasping incessantly, two things that never cultivate peace.

As women of faith, we are called to depend on God in everything. Psalm 37:5 reads, "Commit your way to the Lord; trust in him, and he will act."

Depending on someone else is a foreign and perhaps crazy idea in a society that champions a self-sufficient woman. Our culture trumpets the message that there is more power to the woman who can take care of herself, pay her own bills, and doesn't need a man to do things for her. "Miss Independent" doesn't need to depend on anyone; she is self-sufficient, and this is what gives her strength! As women of faith, we live out a belief that stands in stark contrast to these ideas. We are called to live the reality that it is actually *in* depending on another that we derive our strength. In fact, we are strongest when we are totally dependent on God. We are called to trust him with every aspect of our lives, to surrender our own plans and be open to him, and to love him with all our hearts. As scripture says, "Trust in the LORD with all your heart, and do not rely on your own insight. In all your ways acknowledge him, and he will make straight your paths" (Proverbs 3:5–6).

I always had the same reaction to this concept when I was younger: "Yeah. Depend on God. Trust him. Mhmm. I want to do that, but what does that even look like? How do I do that in my daily life?"

Here's what I have learned: Dependence on God starts the very moment I wake up in the morning. I am not a morning person *at all*, so it takes a lot of effort to remember that every time I wake up, God has given me the gift of another day that was not promised to me. I begin every morning by making an offering of my day to him. I thank him for a new day and offer the day ahead to him, entrusting both the big and the little things to his heart. I invite God into my day because God doesn't force himself into our days—we have to invite him to be a part of our lives. We have to open our hearts to let him know that we want help with recognizing his presence and seeing where he is working and moving. God is always present, but it takes an intentional openness to be able to recognize this.

When we give each day to God, we are inviting him into our lives more fully, and we are able to surrender to a dependence on his will and his strength throughout the day. When we go through our days—no matter how completely mundane, totally exciting, or absolutely terrible they may be—we can stay in tune with the heart of God. We can pray throughout the day, in between classes or during the work day, keeping in conversation with God as we would a friend. We can call on God in a difficult situation with a friend or a stranger and ask him, "Help me to show your love to this person right now." You don't always have to kneel or fold your hands in order to connect in prayer with God; you simply have to speak or quietly let God know that you are open and listening to what he wants to say to you, out loud or in your heart. This is living out Psalm 37:5.

Trusting and depending on God takes practice and intentionality. When we practice trusting God in the little things—entrusting every aspect of our day-to-day life to his care—it becomes more natural to trust and depend on him in the big things. When we walk with God in the day-to-day, we learn to love him more, and in learning to love him more, we can grow in our desire to surrender our own plans to him. We can practice a continual openness to what he wants to do in and through our lives.

God offers us the grace to let go of that timeline we made for ourselves, to relinquish our desire to control where we are going and what may happen on the road ahead. When we surrender our plans, we begin to depend on the only One who can be depended upon—to trust that he truly does withhold no good thing from us (see Psalm 84:11). This doesn't mean we are supposed to sit back and refrain from planning ahead in any aspect of our lives, but it means that we should not freak out when plans change or our own plans don't pan out. When we are working toward total dependence on God, we don't lose our peace when the waters of our life get stormy, because we are walking with God and know that he is present in the midst of every joy and every trial. God promises to guide us; he asks us to live with trust and belief in our hearts that he can and will light the way.

. . . .

TAKE ACTION

This week, if you don't do this already, try to make an effort to take thirty seconds when you wake up to say a simple prayer offering your day to God before you check your phone or get out of bed. See how it changes your approach to your day, and stick with it if you want to incorporate it as part of your daily routine!

FIVE

Date with Purpose

I went on my first date when I was in college at the age of eighteen. During all my years in high school, I watched other girls get asked on countless dates and receive innumerable invitations to school dances, and I felt quite invisible standing in the shadows of popular, well-known girls like Heather and Camille. I was not "popular" at all. I was involved in musical theater rather than cheerleading or sports, and while other girls went to football games on Friday nights, I often stayed home with my family because I wanted to. I enjoyed Friday nights with my family eating popcorn and watching movies rather than standing around gossiping and flirting, the main activity happening in the stands at football games, which was about as interesting to me as watching paint dry.

Sometimes I felt as though I was completely missing out on an important aspect of the "high school experience" by not dating throughout high school. However, after I graduated from high school and went to college, I realized how much I was not missing. I had spent most of my time with my friends and family rather than in relationships that would have eventually ended, and that was something I did not regret at all. I was grateful that I had invested in lifelong friendships and focused on my academics, because the time I poured into those reaped beautiful rewards.

Because I did not date in high school, I am frequently asked if I am opposed to dating in high school. My answer to that is twofold. I am not opposed to dating in high school, but I have found that there is an important question that should be paramount when it comes to dating, no matter a woman's age: *Why?*

As women, we have inherent desires to be accepted and loved. We want to feel beautiful, and maybe, if you're like me, the attention of a man makes you feel good. It makes you feel noticed, seen, or wanted, and it satiates that desire, for a brief moment or for an extended period of time, to feel important to someone. These desires to feel accepted and known are not bad things—they are natural to us and should not be squelched or dismissed. These desires, however, have to be directed in the proper way.

When I was in high school, I definitely had the desire to date. I often wished at dances or social events that a guy, any guy at all, would pay attention to me, talk to me, or even just look at me. They never did. I thought the girls who were in relationships looked like they were having fun and mistakenly believed that their relationship status of "taken" made them more important or beautiful than me. But had someone asked me *why* I had such a strong desire to date, I would certainly not have had a good answer. My honest answer probably would have been, "Because

I want to fit in," "Because I would like having a guy around who pays attention to me and makes me feel beautiful," or simply, "I don't know." Now my high school years are behind me, and I can see clearly that these are never good reasons to get into a relationship. This is where the "why" question comes in.

If you feel that desire to date, it can be helpful to ask yourself: Why do I want to date? Is it because I want someone to pay attention to me, or is it because I want to learn more about qualities I would like to find in a future husband? Is it because I want to have a guy to hang out with, or because I want to grow in virtue with someone?

If you are already in a relationship, you can (and should!) ask yourself: Why am I in this relationship? Is this relationship leading me closer to God or away from God? Is there purpose in this relationship—are we headed in a concrete direction—or are we mindlessly hanging out because it's fun or because it's what we have grown comfortable with? It takes maturity to step back and ask yourself these questions. If you are in a relationship in which you know you are settling, if you're being led away from God or it just doesn't have real purpose, it takes even greater maturity and strength to end that relationship.

It takes great bravery to date with purpose and intentionality. But it is also important to remember that dating isn't supposed to be a super-serious quest to find out if the guy is *the one* as quickly as possible. I get e-mails from sixteen-year-old girls sharing with me that they think they've found *the one*. With respect to all women, it is unlikely that you will find your future husband in high school. Many women do not find their spouse in college, either. This is not a bad thing! Discerning marriage through dating is a process that has no magic formula. Dating should be something that is enjoyable and lighthearted, gradually growing more serious over time.

My husband and I had a lot of fun spending time together and getting to know one another when we were dating, but we were always aware of the why. We were dating to discern if it was God's will for us to get married, and through that process I came to find that my husband is a man of incredible faith, character, and virtue, who would make a kind, loving, and selfless husband and father for potential children. The *why* was always of paramount importance in our process of dating and engagement that eventually led to our marriage.

It takes bravery not to settle for any guy who comes along in order to fulfill that desire to be paid attention to. It takes courage to keep your standards high. It takes strength to step back and ask yourself: *Why?* This requires a strong sense of self-awareness. You need to reflect on your true motives and desires, which is not easy to do. Yet when you implement this question in your life, you prevent yourself from wasting time in meaningless relationships that you're not meant to be in. You are consistently reminded not to settle. You are free to date with good purpose rather than "just because."

Our world is extremely focused on romantic relationships and often puts them on a pedestal as a trophy to be earned. However, we can't forget that relationships are not the end-all and be-all of life. They are not the most important thing, and pursuing them is not worthy of every ounce of our time, energy, and focus. Every woman has a different path, and I know many incredible women who went on their first date when they were in their twenties. Perhaps you've never been on a date, and the thought of being asked on your first date in your twenties makes you want to cry! Take heart. Women who date with purpose do not typically go on as many dates as women who don't. When your standards are high, you will not meet a plethora of men who meet those standards, but great men *are* out there. And no matter your path, always remember that you are no less spectacular than the girls who have the attention of many guys or who get asked to dances by multiple guys or who get engaged before college is over. Receiving the affections of men will never say anything about who you are. You are beautiful, amazing, and wonderful in every way—you don't *become* those things when a guy tells you that you are those things. Boyfriend or not, fiancé or not, husband or not—you are, and will always be, spectacular.

Intentionality in dating is so uncommon yet so worthwhile. Cultivating this intentionality and self-awareness in the way we approach dating and relationships is a concrete way we can choose to love ourselves. When we choose to date with purpose, we give ourselves clear direction instead of wandering around aimlessly, grasping at attention or love, or getting carried away in dead-end pseudo-relationships that are not good for our hearts in any way. The responsibility of taking care of our hearts rests in our hands—we just have to choose to find deep within ourselves the courage to do it.

. . . .

TAKE ACTION

If you are experiencing a desire to date, spend some time with that question: *Why?*

If you are currently in a dating relationship, also spend time with that question: *Why?*

Reflect on your motives and desires, either in your heart or in a journal.

SIX

Just Keep Swimming

"You can't start the next chapter of your life if you keep rereading the last one."

My little sister, Gracie, said this out loud to me one day, reading an inspirational quote she saw on Pinterest. The words came out of her mouth and pierced me right in the heart. I realized: *I am too often a rereader.* Perhaps you can commiserate. Maybe you are a rereader, too.

I often encounter common traits among the women I meet through my travels and conversations, and self-criticism tops the list—we can be really hard on ourselves. (I'm definitely including myself in this one!)

There are a few truths that I think are important to go over here. You and I are both human beings. We are sinners who make mistakes. We mess up, we say the wrong thing, and we hurt other people either intentionally or unintentionally. I have made countless mistakes, and it is an important and healthy life skill to be able to look at, revisit, or consider past mistakes in order to grow. Growing from the past and making positive changes is a very productive, healthy, and intelligent thing to do.

However, if you're like me, you may struggle with falling into the trap of living in the past and constantly dwelling on your mistakes and failures. This struggle manifests in thinking and rethinking and mulling over all our shortcomings and mistakes and allowing that to affect our hearts and our souls negatively. I have spent so much time in my life thinking about how I have let people down or made big mistakes. Sometimes I even lose sleep over it, lying awake in my bed at night with tears falling on my pillow and burgeoning regret in my heart. This obsession with failures and shortcomings slowly starts to steal our peace and cause us to forget about the love and mercy of God. Our God is merciful and kind—and he wants us to be merciful and kind with ourselves when we make mistakes and commit to change. We are works in progress—not perfect people. Expecting perfection of ourselves is an unrealistic demand that we will never be able to meet.

Then there's the nasty trap of believing that if you fail, that makes you a failure. I certainly fall into this thinking too often; it is rare that I remember the things I have accomplished or have been happy about before I remember the ways I have fallen short or the dumb things I've said or the people I have completely let down. I dwell on things I wish I could have done better or things I wish had turned out differently. I spend far too much time remembering the ways I have disappointed others, and I let this disappointment in myself convince me that I am a total failure. This is something I work on changing every day because this does not magnify God or his merciful love in any way.

Here's what I have learned after too many years of beating myself up, and I want you to allow this truth to soak into your heart so deeply that you never forget it: Failing does not make you a failure. Failing, messing up, and making mistakes is part of life. We are imperfect, messy humans who will fall and fall again. Some mistakes will be small, and some may be huge. This is a normal facet of what it means to be a human being.

The beauty of life is that we can always select our *response* to our mistakes and failures.

We can allow them to cause us to despair and pity ourselves, or we can allow them to propel us to try again. We always get to choose our direction—forward or backward. We can dwell in the past, or we can keep swimming forward in life. We choose whether or not we will follow God's promptings in scripture: "Do not remember the former things, or consider the things of old. I am about to do a new thing; now it springs forth, do you not perceive it?" (Isaiah 43:18–19a). We always have a choice.

Dwelling on our mistakes allows a dark cloud to loom over days or seasons of our lives. Beating ourselves up incessantly is not what God has in mind for his daughters, because this dwelling and overthinking and obsessing does not speak at all to the Good News of a God who forgives, a God who invites us to pick ourselves back up and run to him to receive his mercy. There are times in life when we're so mad at ourselves for messing up, so disgusted by our inability to make good choices or to stop falling into that pattern of sin, that we feel as though God must be mad at us, too. We may imagine God saying things to us such as, "Why can't you get anything right? What is wrong with you? Haven't you learned your lesson *yet*?" Perhaps we imagine God speaking to us in that way because it's how we habitually speak to ourselves, or because it's the way someone—a parent, sibling, or teacher—frequently spoke to us when we were growing up. This is never the language or response of a loving God. The heart of God doesn't overflow with criticism, harsh words, or reminders of past mistakes—it overflows with gentleness, kindness, and an offering of his mercy. How do I know this? If God was harsh and critical, Jesus would've looked at the woman caught in adultery (see John 8:1–11) and said, "Really? Seriously? You should be ashamed of yourself." He didn't. He looked on her with love and didn't condemn her, but rather said, "Woman, where are they? Has no one condemned you? . . . Neither do I condemn you. Go your way, and from now on do not sin again" (John 8:10–11). He looked on her with peace, forgave her sin, and lovingly commanded her to change her ways.

When we embrace our humanity and the fact that we will not get everything right the first time or all the time, we are then able to get back up after a fall, to dive back into our lives, open to learning from our mistakes and turning to God the Father for forgiveness. We are ready to carry on forward to try again. We can continually decide to keep going forward with grace and peace in our hearts, trusting in a God who forgives and who makes all things new, so that, as Dory in *Finding Nemo* said, we can just keep swimming, swimming, swimming.

. . . .

TAKE ACTION

Is there a place in your life where you are standing still
or looking back because of regretful dwelling on your
past failures and mistakes? Ask God to help you to stop
rereading and to be open to his mercy and love. If you
feel you need to forgive yourself, ask God to help you do
that. Ask him to help you make the conscious decision
to stop dwelling and instead look forward.

SEVEN

Find Your Gaggle

I have a love-hate relationship with geese. First of all, I am highly allergic to them. I cannot be near anything made of their feathers (also known as "down," which is used to make the most luxurious and comfy blankets and pillows—sad, I know). Fancier hotels often have down in all of their bedding, and so when I stay in nicer hotels, I always have to call the front desk to have my room completely defeathered. It's a big headache of a process!

Geese, however, have taught me more about friendship than I ever thought a bird could teach me about anything. You may know that geese fly south for the winter. They migrate to survive changes in seasons, and they fly in a community that is headed in the same direction. If you have ever watched geese traveling for the winter, you will find them flying in groups through the sky in a "V" formation. When geese fly in this V, each goose flaps its wings and creates an uplift for the goose behind it. They travel as a team, with different geese taking turns leading the group, and they trade positions in the V to help geese who may be exhausted or sickly. Collectively, the geese are able to travel much farther than if they were to travel the distance alone.

Within our makeup as humans, we were created by God with deep longing for intimacy with others. We were made for unity and community, as Jesus called us to community in John 13:34: "Just as I have loved you, you also should love one another." We crave friendship, and we long to be known deeply. This is a natural part of who we are. As Christians, we are called to be like geese. We are called to the community, friendship, and love that we see geese exhibit in the way they fly.

As Christians it is essential to our journey to find people who are going in the same direction as us. When we decide to live a life of wholehearted faith, everything changes. Life becomes more than some means to happiness and fulfillment. Life has purpose when we choose to build God's kingdom here on earth, be God's hands and feet, and fulfill the individual call he has placed on each of our lives. When we encounter Christ and decide to apply faith in our lives in a deep and real way, our priorities change.

It is difficult to cultivate true community and deep friendship with people who don't share what is most important to you. Does this mean you can only have friends who agree with everything you believe and live their faith in the same way that you do? No, of course not. We could never evangelize if everyone who loved Jesus just stuck together in a small, exclusive bubble! Jesus spent time with tax collectors and prostitutes, many people who didn't at all live or believe what he was teaching. The friends you choose do not necessarily have to share your beliefs, but if your ultimate destination is heaven, it is very important to cultivate deep friendships and community with others who are trying to get there, too.

A community is a group of people sharing common characteristics—a group of people who hold you accountable and support and motivate you to become the best version of yourself. Community is a means for us to hold one another accountable in our walks of faith—to encourage, support, and uplift one another like geese do, when times are great and when times are very challenging.

Community and friendship is also an avenue by which God shows his face to us during the most difficult trials of life. When I was in middle school, my mom was diagnosed with stage–two breast cancer. It was an extremely difficult season for my family. For many months, people from our school and church community would show up every night with a hot dinner that they prepared for our family. Friends constantly lifted us up in prayer and came to pray with us. The people in our community "flew in front of us," as geese do when members of their community are sick or tired, so that we could continue to persevere through the journey of my mom's illness. That was community. That was God showing his face to us. Jesus didn't show up on our front porch with Italian food from Buca di Beppo every night. He used other people to do that—he used community to show us his love.

One of the biggest troubles I find among women is that they feel as though they are trapped in a group of friends who do not support them, who put them down, or in friendships that feel

completely superficial. It is imperative to keep in mind throughout your life that a group of friends is not some tattoo you cannot
remove. If you are unhappy with your friends—if your friends
are pressuring you to do things you don't want to do or if you
see them heading in a direction you don't want to go—it is never
too late to find new friends. It is not ever worthwhile to waste
your time and energy with people who do not support you in
growing into who you want to be. In living your faith, it can be
difficult to have patience in finding friends who share your core
values, but it is a worthwhile endeavor.

When I was at ASU, I tried to build friendships with the people in my classes. Some of them were nice people, but I quickly
found that it was difficult to find people who cared deeply about
the same things as I did or shared my core values. I thought that
it did not matter that much, that I could still be great friends
with some of my classmates even though we had major differ-
ences in the things we cared about. After a while, I found that
these friendships were not really fulfilling me. I wanted to have
conversations about my faith and learn more about my faith in
conversations with friends. I wanted to spend time with people
who could pray with me and for me, and that was not something
I could share with these people.

So after far too long of trying to develop deep friendships
with people who didn't share my faith, I went to the Newman
Center on campus and found a wonderful woman named
Andrea. Andrea shared with me that she was part of a women's
group that met every Thursday at her friend's house, and she
invited me to join them at their next gathering. The first night

they were talking about St. Joan of Arc and the ways we could be inspired by her life. I breathed a sigh of relief. God had graciously led me to a group of women who cared deeply about what I cared about, and I knew that was a group in which I could cultivate true, deep, authentic friendships within a loving community of women. This was a game changer for my college experience. After being introduced to all the women, I developed friendships with many of them that continued throughout college. My only regret was not going to the Newman Center earlier!

Finding great friends as a young woman of faith requires patience, perseverance, and intentionality. It is unlikely that if you ask God for a great group of women to be friends with, he will drop them right in your lap. Often we have to seek these things out with determination. But when we are purposeful and intentional about who we surround ourselves with, our whole life is impacted and uplifted in an overwhelmingly positive way. We realize the great depth that friendships can have when we walk alongside our brothers and sisters in Christ who can uplift us along the journey. We become like geese—those wonderful birds who by their lives provide us not only with comfy duvets but also with top-notch advice on friendship.

. . . .

TAKE ACTION

Step back to take a good, long look at the friends you have surrounded yourself with. Are they a good influence on you? Do they support you and love you for who you are and who you know God is calling you to be? If not, consider how you can make some changes or work toward cultivating friendships with others who will.

EIGHT

Choose Chastity

When I was a teenager and heard the word "chastity," I often confused it with the word "abstinence." I thought that chastity meant saving sex for marriage, which I have since come to find is a common misconception. Chastity is a virtue that is about much more than saving sex for marriage. This virtue is about the purity of our bodies but also encompasses the purity of our hearts and minds. Married people live chastity, and priests and nuns practice chastity. Chastity involves living out our sexuality in the beautiful and healthy way God designed it, and it is also about what we consume with our eyes, our ears, and our hearts.

Chastity is the virtue that compels us to step back and look at the whole of our lives and see what is and is not contributing to the purity of our hearts. We don't have to look far to see that many books, movies, and social media posts being presented to us every day are full of filth and do nothing to aid us in living the virtue of chastity. Popular television shows are filled with vulgarity, sexual promiscuity, and profanity. Many songs on the radio focus on hookups, drunkenness, and drug use. The fact that vulgarity and promiscuity are considered by so many to be humorous, entertaining, and normal in our world today is very sad and, if we're looking at it realistically, really pathetic. These themes are portrayed as harmless and funny. The thing about vulgarity and inappropriate content is that the more we consume it, the more we become desensitized to it. It is similar to something like consumption of coffee; someone who drinks coffee daily will become much less affected by the caffeine than someone who drinks a cup once a week.

In her *Essays on Woman*, Edith Stein, also known as St. Teresa Benedicta of the Cross, spoke about how as women we are to awaken within ourselves a "joyful emotion for authentic beauty and goodness and disgust for that which is base and vulgar." Put simply, if we are pursuing holiness, we should have an *aversion to vulgarity*. It is supposed to disgust us rather than draw us in or make us laugh, because of our inherent desires for goodness and beauty.

As humans, we seek beauty, and we crave it. Who isn't awestruck by a beautiful sunset? Who isn't moved by a beautiful piece of music or witnessing a random act of kindness performed by a stranger? We have an innate desire for and attraction to what is beautiful and good (see *CCC,* 2002). This desire for goodness ultimately causes us to seek God, who is goodness himself. It is a very good thing that beauty causes us to seek God because the more we seek God, the more we find him. And the more we find God in our lives, the more fulfilled we are.

However, when we grow desensitized to the ugly things of our world that don't contribute to the purity of our hearts and minds, it can disrupt our ability to experience our deep longing to consume beauty and goodness. If we are surrounded by the muck and mire of the things of this world, we may forget altogether how much better we feel when we surround ourselves with good and uplifting things. This does not mean that we can never watch a movie or listen to music ever again. We simply have to cultivate a discerning eye and ear for what is good for us and what is not. My question for you is this: Are there things in your life that you are consuming that are not contributing to the purity of your mind and heart? Are there movies or shows you are watching, music you are listening to, or accounts that you are following that are hindering your pursuit of the virtue of chastity? If we are going to magnify the love of Christ to the world, we have to rid our lives of the things that do nothing to uplift our hearts and minds and that desensitize us to the base and vulgar.

Chastity also encompasses our physical sexuality and living it out in a beautiful and pure way. We live in a world in which sex is portrayed as meaningless. The culture tells us that it is not unusual to have sex on a first date, with a guy friend, or with men you do not know. Perhaps you've heard one or ten people in your life spout off the lie that "sex is not a big deal." The idea the world is constantly promoting that sex is as meaningless as ordering Chinese takeout (yum, orange chicken) makes the decision to save sex for marriage a completely unconventional and altogether radical decision in this day and age.

I decided to save sex for marriage when I was sixteen years old. It is important to note that I do not believe that my decision to save sex for marriage makes me "better" than any woman who has chosen otherwise. I made this decision as a teenager, and now I write this to you many years later with a sparkly wedding band on my left hand. When I made this decision, I did not fully realize how much my pretty wedding band was intertwined with living out the virtue of chastity in my own life.

On my wedding day, December 30, 2015, a sweet young Dutch man with dark curls stood facing me on a red carpeted altar, and he looked me in the eyes and said vows out loud in front of all our friends and family, ending with this sentence: "I will love you and honor you all the days of my life."

This man, my husband, Daniël, vowed to love me forever. After he stated these vows, he placed a wedding ring on my hand and said, "I give you this ring as a sign of *my* love and fidelity." My sparkling ring is not a sign of my promise to my husband; it is a symbol of his promise to me. It is a sign of his love and fidelity—fidelity being his faithfulness to me as his wife. This ring is a tangible sign that my husband has promised to be present to me, through joyful times and difficult ones, in sickness and health. It is a sign that he will celebrate with me on my best days and weep with me on my worst days. It is a sign that I am truly, fully, and deeply loved.

If God's call and plan for your life is marriage, the man who vows his entire life to you and places your wedding ring on your hand in front of all your friends and family is the only man who deserves the honor of having you give all of yourself to him. The pursuit of chastity is a worthwhile endeavor for every person, no matter the specific vocation to which you are called.

Your body is sacred (see *CCC*, 364). Sex is a sacred thing, but our culture—made up of celebrities and magazines and music and other people whom we look to for their opinions—will tell you that if you're not sleeping around or having sex with your boyfriend, you are uncool or behind everyone else. I knew these messages to be untrue as a young woman, trying to live chastity, but it wasn't until after I was married that I came to find out just how untrue these messages are.

There was a deep freedom that I found in marrying a man who didn't require that we have sex before marriage. You may find that if you are choosing to live chastity, it can be a deal breaker for guys time and time again, and that can be frustrating. However, I want you to know that every time a guy walks away because you tell him that you are choosing chastity, he is doing you a favor; it is not worthwhile to date men who want to take from you what does not belong to them. You are worth so much more.

When I met Daniël and shared with him that I was saving sex for marriage, I knew he was a good man and was also stunned when his response was, "Great. Me too." I knew that no matter if we got married or not, he was a man who wanted to date me to get to know my heart and mind rather than my body. We got married two years and eight months after we met, and as I walked down the aisle on my wedding day, I had an unwavering awareness and knowledge that I was loved for who I am. I knew that the man at the end of the aisle saw the beauty of my heart, my gifts, and my willingness to love—and he didn't need any part of my body to help him decide that he wanted me to be his wife and vow his life to me forever.

Women often share with me their fears about their wedding night if they have saved their virginity for their husband. What I found within my own wedding night was that I had nothing to fear. I wasn't concerned about Daniël judging my ability to be "good at" physical intimacy—after all, I had just trusted him with *my entire life* when I declared my vows at our wedding. I knew that my giving of my body to my husband wasn't about my abilities but about my openness to love him and become one person with him in the context of a sacrament. I didn't feel awkward, because I knew he didn't marry me for what I can give or do—he married me for who I am.

The morning after our wedding, we had breakfast in the hotel restaurant, and it was the first morning that we had woken up as one person within the sacrament. It was the first morning of our new life together, and I felt no regret. I didn't have any fear or questioning that so many of my friends expressed they felt after sex with a boyfriend or guy they did not know. I looked at the brand-new wedding ring on my left hand, deeply aware that I was sitting across the table from a man who would never leave me, and I felt loved. I felt safe. I felt free.

Bravery is required in the decision to save sex for marriage, but there is also bravery required in deciding to change your life if you have made decisions that you regret. Perhaps you have decided to or have been pressured to have sex or be overly physical with a boyfriend, or friend, or guys you do not know. If this is the case, know that you are not alone. If you hold regret about choices you have made or the pressure you have given into, the good news is that it is never too late to change your life. Countless women have vulnerably shared with me about the way choosing to engage in casual sex made them feel—many have expressed deep regret, sorrow, and feelings of emptiness. That is because sex was beautifully designed to be experienced within the indissoluble vow of marriage (see *CCC*, 2360).

It is never too late, in any aspect of our lives where we know we are not making the best choices for ourselves, to decide we want to make a change. If you have not saved sex for marriage, hear me very clearly when I tell you that *it does not reduce your inherent value and worth.* It does not lessen the sacredness of your body or your sexuality—but if you want to reflect God's love through the way you treat your body, you must make a change. You may think, "Well, I have given away my virginity already, so it doesn't matter anymore anyway." Yes, it does. Your body will always be a sacred, beautiful, valuable thing. You cannot lessen your value. Your sexuality will always be sacred. You are still infinitely loved by Christ. The boundless and tender mercy and love of God the Father will always be available to you.

When women in scripture who are struggling with sin come to Jesus, he always meets them with love and compassion, and he always gives them a firm command—go, and sin no more. He doesn't say, "Well, maybe you should think about changing your life." The command is firm, clear, and deeply loving. When we have not lived in a way that glorifies God with our sexuality, he commands us in this very same way, because he desires what is best for us—true and lasting fulfillment. He knows that true and lasting fulfillment can be found when we incorporate chastity into every aspect of our lives.

Making that kind of change is not easy and requires great intentionality. It requires courage. Sometimes it takes writing a letter to God or to yourself about the change you are making, putting it down on paper in black and white in order to make this decision concretely and wholeheartedly. It may require a very direct and thorough conversation with your boyfriend, or a very clear-cut conversation with a guy friend with whom you have had an inappropriate physical relationship. It requires that you stand up for yourself with your words and firmly say, "I've decided to make a change in my life," and explain what that change looks like. It is not easy, but it is worth it. The right men will respect your choice to change; walk away from the men who don't. Only you have the power to change your life in this way, and I firmly believe that you can because I have seen numerous friends of mine who did not save sex for marriage decide to change their life and wait until their wedding day. I tell you with confidence that even though it was challenging, each of them would tell you that they are so glad they recommitted themselves to a life of chastity.

The world will tell you that living out the virtue of chastity will hold you back from freedom. What the world does not know is that the virtue of chastity and freedom go hand in hand. Chastity is a virtue that sets us free from worry, stress, regret, and sorrow. Practicing chastity gives you the confidence to know a guy is dating you for who you are, not for what you can give or do. This virtue frees us to live in the purity and radical beauty that

God created us for. It awakens within us that "joyful emotion for authentic beauty and goodness," eyes and hearts wide open to experience authentic love, overflowing joy, and lasting peace.

. . . .

TAKE ACTION

Are there TV shows, movies, social media accounts you are following, or other media in your life that are not contributing to the purity of your heart? Consider making the choice to cut those things out of your life in order to pursue the virtue of chastity.

If you are not happy with or are regretful about the choices you have made with your sexuality, consider the possibility of making a promise to yourself or to God to choose differently from today forward. Write it down somewhere, or make an honest prayer to God and ask him to give you the courage to choose differently.

NINE

Be Open to the Jump

In 2014, I jumped off the top of the World Cup soccer stadium in Durban, South Africa. The jump is called the World's Tallest Rope Swing. I was speaking and singing at events in the country, and some of the locals had let my friends and me know that it was an exhilarating experience that could not be missed before we left the city. I am not typically one who gets excited about extreme sports, heights, or other things of the heart-pounding nature, but I thought to myself, "I could skip this, sit in the stadium seats, and watch everyone else do it, or I could be open to it and have the time of my life." In a moment of courage, I chose to participate.

Every participant in this jump has to climb 550 stairs while attached by a rope to the side of the staircase in order to make it to the top of the stadium where you jump. Once you reach the top, you must climb backward down a ladder onto a metal catwalk. There are three men who greet you there to secure your harness and see you off on your jump. I was quite nervous, as I had never done anything like this before.

The guy standing to my right attached my harness and said in a thick South African accent, "We will count, 3, 2, 1, and you must jump."

Then he said something that left me breathless: "If you don't jump, we will push you."

My stomach dropped. Shove me off a ledge high in the sky? No, thank you! I didn't want to be pushed. I wanted to feel the thrill of jumping off myself!

So I stepped outside of my comfort zone, and I hopped off that ledge. The thrill was more exciting and intense than anything I'd ever done in my life. After jumping, I was in free fall for a few seconds, and then the rope caught me, and I swung across the entire stadium. It was incredible. I was so glad I chose to do it, as it is an experience I will remember forever.

Life offers many possibilities for exhilarating adventures. It is good to get out of your comfort zone and try new things, but there is never a man standing to your right who tells you he will shove you out of your comfort zone if you don't jump yourself! We must choose to push ourselves and take risks. You have to decide to go on that retreat, attend that networking event put on by your university, or take that photography class you've been thinking about. It's rarely the case that someone will force you to do it.

Comfort zones are, admittedly, very cozy places. My personal comfort zone is like the elaborate forts my sisters and I used to build in our childhood bedroom—full of soft pillows and stuffed animals and safety. I like being in my comfort zone. I can rest and relax and be unchallenged there. Maybe you're like me, and you like what you are familiar with, but what we are familiar with doesn't often challenge us to grow in any way. The familiar doesn't push us to try new things, to realize our capabilities, or to experience the vibrancy of life. It is when we step out of our comfort zones that we can begin to grow and learn new things about ourselves and others.

There is one nagging question that has often kept me from trying new things and venturing out into the uncomfortable and unknown: What if?

What if I look like a fool trying to play that sport? What if I don't like the cooking class? What if I go on the retreat, and I'm the only person who doesn't know anybody? What if I play my original song at the open-mic night, and nobody thinks it's any good? What if? This question can almost start to become like handcuffs, keeping our hands locked together in fear so that we don't try anything new or take a chance on anything unfamiliar.

I had what-ifs going through my head as I climbed the staircase to the jump. What if the harness breaks? What if it's more frightening than I thought it would be? What I decided to do was turn my what-if into a why-not. Why not see how fun it could be? Why not try something new? Why not try something exhilarating while I'm in a country I may never visit again? I pushed through the spirit of what-if and into the spirit of why-not, got to the top of the stairs, and jumped—and I loved it. Even if I had found it completely unenjoyable, I would have survived to live another day. If we try new things and don't like them, we can always decide not to do them again. My parents have helped me understand this over and over again in my life. If you sign up for that photography class and you find you don't like it, you're not stuck there forever! It's always worth a try!

Anyone can live their life in a safe, dull place of comfort and never do anything that pushes them to grow and change. That is and will always be an option for your life. But there are many beautiful opportunities to seize in life, and often they feel scary and require a bold decision on our part to say, "I'm going to try this, and if it goes well, great. If it doesn't go well or I don't like it, that's okay, too. I will have learned from the experience and will have grown as a person, and that is always a good thing."

Let's challenge ourselves to open our hearts to the adventure of life and give ourselves permission to take risks. Let's push through the fear of the things that seem scary but could provide great opportunity to grow and experience new things. There won't be a South African man who threatens to shove you to do it. Instead, you'll always get the thrilling opportunity to choose to jump yourself. You will always have the option to hold yourself back with the question "What if?" or to free yourself by asking, "Why not?" Living in that second question continually helps me be open to new life experiences, just as it helped me be open to jumping off that ledge in the sky. It can help you be open to the jump in your life, too. Why not?

. . . .

TAKE ACTION

What is something you've always wanted to try? Maybe something immediately comes to mind, or perhaps you have to think for a while. Whatever you think of, give it a go! Sign up for that class, that league, that retreat—buy the equipment or the ticket to make it happen! Give yourself permission to jump!

TEN

Honor Those Who Love You Most

A few years ago, I was sitting in the Minneapolis airport preparing to board a flight. The woman next to me made a phone call and began to talk. "Hey, it's Mom. I've been trying to call to see how you are doing, to see if you are doing OK." I could hear the muffled voice of a young woman on the other end, and she paused for a while. "Fine, OK. I'm sorry it's so inconvenient for me to call. I'll stop trying." She ended the call, obviously frustrated and annoyed, but I could see in her face that she was heartbroken. She was a mother, trying to reach out to her daughter, and the door was firmly slammed in her face as she was made to feel like a complete inconvenience and a total bother. I felt so sad for her.

As we navigate life as young women, tensions with our parents or primary caretakers can run extremely high. We are becoming individuals with our own opinions and ideals, and that can cause some major butting of heads, some serious blowout fights, and some deep wounds. The only perfect parent-child relationship was between Jesus and his mother!

While your relationship with your parents or the person who raised you may sometimes be strained or difficult to navigate, God is not vague about how we are to treat our parents. He values the loving of one's parents so much that he made it the fourth commandment. He instructs us to *honor* them, and he instructs us to do this before he instructs us not to kill. This is not something to be brushed aside. Scripture is filled with instructions on how we are to treat our parents. Proverbs 1:8 states, "Hear, my child, your father's instruction, and do not reject your mother's teaching." In Matthew 15:3–4, Jesus reminds us of the fourth commandment: "[Jesus] answered them, 'And why do you break the commandment of God for the sake of your tradition? For God said, "Honor your father and your mother."'" But what does it mean to live out the fourth commandment to honor your father and mother? What does that look like in our day-to-day lives?

Honoring the people who raised you can be lived out in a variety of ways. It is important to recognize that these people have poured out more for you in your life than you will probably ever be able to comprehend. Someone had to feed you and do your laundry and take care of you when you were small; someone had to pick you up from school or drive you around to various activities. The love and sacrifice that it takes to raise a child is something that could never be captured in words, and this is something we can forget very easily.

Beyond this recognition, honoring your parents calls you to be respectful in your words, thoughts, and actions—even when they annoy you, even when you disagree with their rules, standpoints, or opinions. If you disagree with their rules, you can honor them by stepping back to ask the reasoning behind their rules to facilitate respectful dialogue and conversation rather than just shutting down or shutting them out. We are called to speak to them with respectful words and tone. We are called to honor them even when we're tired of their calls to check on us, like the woman's daughter on the other end of the phone at the airport. In this moment, this woman's daughter hurt her by her actions. It is also important to remember that our actions can hurt our parents. Our capacity to hurt them is beyond what we will ever be able to grasp unless we have children ourselves. God instructs us to honor our parents' desire to connect with us and talk with us in something as simple as a phone call or an invitation to lunch.

Another avenue by which we can honor our parents is by spending time with them. When we spend time with people, we show them that we value them and their presence in our life. When we make the conscious decision to put our phones away and thoroughly engage in our conversations with people, we show them that they are important to us. This can be difficult to do with our parents when we are in high school and college. You may feel as though free time is hard to come by and that you want to spend the free time that you do have with your friends. You may simply be completely bothered by your parents, and it's not human nature for us to want to spend time with people who annoy us. Whatever your situation may be, carving out time to spend with your parents—even if it's an hour-long coffee date with your mom or dad—shows that you care. It shows that they are important to you and that you don't take for granted the love and time they have poured into raising you. It shows them that you have not forgotten them in the midst of your busy life. Never undervalue the power of spending quality time with people you love.

It may be easy to talk about honoring our parents in theory, but each of us has a different situation with our parents. I am blessed with the two best parents I ever could have asked God for, and I don't take that for granted, because I have friends who do not know their parents or who experience great suffering because one of their parents has passed away. I know that your situation with your parents may not be ideal. Perhaps you were not raised by your biological parents, perhaps one of your parents left your family, or perhaps you've always lived with both your parents but you have never truly felt as though they really care about you.

Only you know what your home life has looked like as you have grown up, which can make living out the fourth commandment something that is not completely clear-cut. It may be that you do not feel as though you can live out the fourth commandment, because one or both of your parents have not ever been present to you in your life. One of the ways you can honor your parents, despite less-than-ideal circumstances, is by praying diligently for them. It is possible that they need incredible conversion of heart or life. You can show God that you honor them by keeping them as part of your daily prayers, praying that their hearts be changed, softened, and that they may turn to God in their need or in their suffering. Prayer is a beautiful gift you can give to someone without their even knowing, and it's a way to honor your parents if your circumstances do not allow you to spend time with them or even speak with them.

Honoring our parents is not a walk in the park, but it is something God calls us to do. In those moments or seasons or conversations when you are not getting along with your parents, humbly ask God to help you step back and respond with respect and love. If you disagree with their rules, ask God to help you understand why they may have these rules in place. Pray for your parents. Recognize that while they are not perfect, you are not either. Have mercy on them, and in all things, make every attempt to honor them and their beautiful, sacrificial love for you.

· ·

TAKE ACTION

Many times we call our parents to ask for something or to vent or complain. This time, call your parent or primary caretaker and ask them about their life and how they are doing, and listen to their response. See how they react!

ELEVEN

Give It All You've Got

I was fifteen years old when I started dusting glass and filing patient folders at a small eyeglasses store in a little city called Woodland Hills, California. I applied for a work permit in order to get the job and worked there for my junior and senior years of high school. After senior year, I got a job as a hostess at California Pizza Kitchen, which worked in my favor as I love barbecue chicken pizza. I also got a job as an attraction host at Universal Studios, taking people through the Backdraft attraction. I was seventeen years old and fully in charge of activating and controlling the switchboard for a massive pyrotechnics display in the last room of the attraction tour. I wasn't nervous while I was doing it, but thinking about the magnitude of that responsibility *terrifies* me now! It was crazy!

I always enjoyed working hard and getting a paycheck for all my hard work. I come from a family filled with people who have worked really hard and had little to nothing handed to them. My wonderful grandfather grew up in an orphanage. During the Depression, his father left the family, and his mother could not afford to take care of her children alone. She made the painful but necessary decision to send them to a Catholic orphanage in Philadelphia to be raised, educated, and cared for, so my grandfather was raised by nuns. He received his education through the high school the nuns ran, and upon his graduation day, he was given a one-dollar bill and a rosary. It was all the nuns could send the young boys into the world with, along with education and faith. He worked different trade jobs throughout his teenage years and into young adulthood. Ultimately, he ended up being hired as a secretary for a very influential lawyer and working tirelessly to become a lawyer himself. The hard work he poured into his life is both incalculable and inspiring. I am grateful to have been instilled with the values of hard work and dedication through the example of my grandfather, my parents, and many other members of my family.

Scripture reveals that working hard, with faith as part of our hard work, is part of God's plan for us. Colossians 3:23–24 says, "Whatever your task, put yourselves into it, as done for the Lord and not for your masters, since you know that from the Lord you will receive the inheritance as your reward; you serve the Lord Christ." This means that we can offer everything we do to God—whether it's studying, working as an executive at a big company, leading an important meeting, raising children, or doing laundry. Working hard at anything in our lives becomes important when we realize that everything we do can give glory to God—yes, even scrubbing toilets, waiting tables, and taking final exams. All we need to do is offer our hard work to God as we do it, saying, "God, I offer this work to you. Help me to give you glory in it."

St. Thérèse of Lisieux lived out a beautiful example of how to give glory to God in every part of life through what she called "the little way." Her little way was a simple and humble dedication to doing her daily duties, finding God in all things, and loving God through every task appointed to her. She dedicated her days and tasks to God and prayed through them. Beyond her work, she even found ways to give glory to God in her annoyances and frustrations by practicing patience with people who frustrated her and biting her tongue when she wanted to say sassy things. She glorified God in everything, and we can, too.

Our culture talks frequently about today's young people as the generation of "entitlement." To be entitled is to hold the belief that we shouldn't have to work hard for things—that we deserve to have those things handed to us "just because." Our call as Christians stands in stark contrast to entitlement. Our call isn't just to sit back and receive—it is to get up and act. We each have a different call that God has placed on our lives, but the golden thread that is weaved through each of our calls is God's desire that we work hard for his glory.

There has never been a community or city transformed by the love of God by people simply sitting around and waiting for it to get done. When clean water lines are built for communities in Africa, it doesn't happen by people sitting around dreaming about it happening. It happens because people have recognized their call to be Christ's hands and feet in the world—to enter into the amazing things God is calling them to. They rise to the occasion, respond to the call, and do it—and they bring glory to God through it all.

In a world full of distractions, however, it can be easy to lose focus and not do the hard work. It's easier to scroll through social media than it is to start a new ministry at church. It's easier to watch a favorite TV show rather than go out to help at a fundraising event for a local pregnancy counseling center. This all circles back to the challenge to live intentionally.

A common thought is that the one and only way we can give glory to God in a career is through ministry work or work in a church or faith setting. This is not true. I take great delight in seeing athletes on TV who have won a big game begin their postgame interview, while wiping away sweat and out of breath, saying, "All glory to God!" You can offer your work to God in any field you may dream of going into. Our world needs hardworking women who love God across all facets of life. We need hardworking, Jesus-following scientists, fashion designers, mothers, teachers, accountants, attorneys, and more. You can do "ministry" and live out your call to greatness in whatever field you choose. There are people in every field of work who are in need of great love, who need to meet someone who can shine the light of Christ into their lives. Every profession in the world can be used as an avenue through which God can work and in which God can be glorified.

I found ways to glorify God in my work at the optical store, at California Pizza Kitchen, and at Universal Studios by praying through my work. As I was filing, I took time to talk to God. As I took people through the pyrotechnics display, I would pick out people to pray for in my heart. My work had nothing to do with Jesus, at least explicitly, but I made a conscious choice to glorify God in it anyway. I decided to work hard and to give it all I had in serving the people God put before me. And you can do exactly that—in everything you do, give thanks, praise, and honor to the God who made you. You can choose to give it all you've got and bring him glory in every moment of your life.

"And whatever you do, in word or deed, do everything in the name of the Lord Jesus, giving thanks to God the Father through him" (Colossians 3:17).

. . . .

TAKE ACTION

Every day this week when you go to work or school, when the day or shift begins, make this simple little prayer: "God, I offer this work to you. Help me bring you glory in it."

TWELVE

Love Yourself

For a few years, I worked as a campus ministry director for a high school in California, and I had one student whom I saw almost every day. Sophia would come to my office each day after school to pass the time before her mom arrived to pick her up. She loved hearing silly stories about my life, like the time I had a secret admirer in college. "People really have secret admirers?" she would ask bashfully, as she giggled and hid behind her long, red hair. "I thought that only happened in the movies!"

Because she was very shy, Sophia struggled to make friends. She often lamented that no one liked her because girls only talked to her about homework and never inquired about her personal life. One afternoon when she seemed particularly down, I struck up a conversation with her to find out what was really going on.

"Name one thing you love about yourself, Sophia," I said, catching her off guard.

"I don't know," she said, immediately turning red. "I have no idea."

"Is there anything you love about yourself?" I asked. She had no response.

I realized in that moment how many girls could sit on the couch in my office and tell me that there is nothing they love about themselves. I challenge young women often to answer this question for me, and so many respond with "I don't know." They cannot look me in the eyes and say, "I love that I am a loyal friend," or "I love that I have a passion for taking care of people." The ability to state these things is not prideful or egotistical; there is a holy confidence that we as young women can live out when we recognize that God gave us incredible characteristics and qualities. If I looked you in the eyes, as I did with Sophia, and asked you to name some things you love about yourself, would you be able to?

If you're anything like me, you can be quick to come up with everything you find wrong about yourself. So often our negative self-talk begins as we get ready in the morning, looking into the mirror and already thinking of the things we see that we wish we could change. That negative self-talk can continue throughout the day as we tell ourselves things we would never say to others! For many women, it is a great challenge to think of one or two things they love about themselves. This poses a great obstacle to reflecting the love of Christ, because it is hard to love others in the way God calls us to—selflessly and wholeheartedly—if we do not first learn to love ourselves, flaws and all. Learning to love who we are, whether that is in our appearance or personality, can be a long and difficult journey, but it is a journey Christ wants to accompany us on so that we can see ourselves the way he does. Christ *wants* you to love yourself in a healthy, beautiful way.

Before we get further into this book, I want you to stop what you are doing and go to the mirror with this book. Are you at the mirror now?

Look at yourself.

Think of three things you love about yourself. Where is there good in your heart? What do you excel at in your life? Is there a certain aspect of your appearance that you like? What are some of your gifts? Look into your eyes and into your soul. What do you love about the soul that you have?

Do not leave the mirror until you can think of three things.

I told Sophia she could not leave my office until she came up with one thing. I ended up having to leave work, and she still couldn't think of anything. So I sent her home with the assignment to think of just one thing.

Do not leave that mirror without three.

In my own high school experience, I didn't feel pretty or as though I had very many friends. One day I was riding home on the bus from our sophomore retreat while some girls were talking about the upcoming homecoming dance. I was listening in when one of the girls turned to me and said, "Don't worry about getting invited. You won't, because you're ugly." I couldn't believe someone would actually say that right to someone's face! Her words really stung me as a fifteen-year-old girl trying to feel beautiful in my own skin.

There were many moments like these when I felt unattractive and unlovable. One day I came across an article in a magazine about daily "mirror affirmations" and how they can change your perspective of yourself. A mirror affirmation involves looking at yourself in the mirror and speaking positive words into your own heart and life. I thought I would give it a try in hopes of feeling better, so I wrote up my own affirmation, and every day I began to look in the mirror and say to myself, "My name is Emily Wilson, and I love and accept myself. My name is Emily Wilson, and I am a beautiful and radiant daughter of God." It felt strange for the first while, but then it started to become easier. The more I continued to say it every day, the more I began to believe it. I truly began to feel a change in the way I felt about myself, simply because of this affirmation. I have encouraged many girls to do this since then, and if loving yourself is something you struggle with, I invite you to do it, too. Look at yourself in the mirror, and speak uplifting words with these two sentences: "My name is _____, and I love and accept myself. My name is _____, and I am a beautiful and radiant daughter of God."

About a year after the conversation we had in my office, I got a text from Sophia. She had been on a life-changing retreat and sent me a text message that said, "I have come to accept who I am, and it is an amazing feeling. I have found that I am a courageous, important, kindhearted girl who affects those around her in whatever she does. These are the qualities and things I like about myself. I can finally give you an answer to your question." I was both astonished and grateful to receive her message. Even though it took a year, she had come to realize the beauty inside of her—the wonderful girl that she is—and that it had nothing to do with her appearance. She saw the beauty she had inside her heart.

Women who are confident and learn to love themselves shine God's love into the heart of every person they encounter. Don't wait a year to begin recognizing and loving who you are right now. It takes effort and prayer, and it is important to remember that loving who God made us to be is not something that happens in one instant or one day—it is a continual process and a journey. I have to remind myself of this often in my own journey of learning and choosing to love myself. Ask God to help you live in the holy confidence that comes from the knowledge that he created you, and that there are so many good and beautiful things about you. Do not wait. Begin today.

· ·

TAKE ACTION

Look in the mirror, and think about those three things you love about yourself. Consider writing them down somewhere so that you can easily remind yourself of them when you're having a hard day or in a season when you are struggling to love the woman God made you to be.

THIRTEEN

Clothe Yourself in Strength

There are two prominent, outright lies about our bodies being fed to us women by our culture. The first lie is that the more skin we show as women, the more powerful we are. The second lie is that revealing clothes will get us what we want—things such as boys, attention, social media "likes," and popularity. Many of the celebrated female celebrities in our world flaunt their bodies on red carpets, in social media, and in magazines. The world trumpets the belief that women who bare it all are actually showing their power and their confidence. We are often told to believe that we can have more of an impact as a woman who flaunts her female figure. As a Christian woman, I believe the exact opposite. Scripture reveals that our bodies are temples of the Holy Spirit: "Or do you not know that your body is a temple of the Holy Spirit within you, which you have from God, and that you are not your own?" (1 Corinthians 6:19).

What does it mean that your body is a temple of the Holy Spirit? That language can be a bit confusing. It means that *God dwells in you.* This is a very important reality. This is why we, as women, are called to purity. The Spirit of God lives within you and me; we are called to keep this in mind always, in everything we do. However, this does not mean that you have to cut out arm-holes in a burlap bag and never wear anything beautiful ever again—because, well, burlap bags are itchy. What this means is that we can reflect that God dwells within us in the way we clothe ourselves; we can outwardly display that we are inherently valuable and possess great dignity. We can outwardly reflect in the way we dress that we know who we are—daughters of the living God.

When I was a teenager attending youth retreats and events, I always felt confused by the questions I was told to ask myself when picking clothes: "Will this outfit lead a guy to have lustful thoughts?" or "Will this outfit help my brother in Christ on his path to purity?" While I wanted to help men on their journey of pursuing purity in their hearts and minds, I was never absolutely certain of the answer to those questions, so I decided to reframe the question. When it came to choosing my clothes, I wanted to be able to ask myself a question that was more practical and helpful for me. I decided to ask myself something I could always answer definitively: "Does this outfit reflect that I am a woman of dignity and value, a woman who knows that God dwells within her?" This question made a lot of sense to me and was—and has always been—very easy to answer when leafing through the racks of cute tops, pants, shorts, or dresses at a store.

Having a consistent awareness of these questions helped me to understand why as a Christian woman I am called to dress modestly. I cover my body because I am, and will always be, a woman of infinite value and dignity. I cover my body not because I am uncomfortable with it or embarrassed by it but because I know that I don't derive my strength from showing my skin. By dressing in a way that shows I am a woman of dignity and infinite value, I indirectly help my brothers in Christ in their fight for purity. This is a win-win situation.

I had to reframe these questions for myself, and I also had to reframe the way I viewed and thought about the word "modesty." There have been times and seasons when I have wrestled with the word "modesty." Modesty is a beautiful and holy virtue that we should continually strive to practice, but there were times when the word made me think of two women in long skirts and turtlenecks knitting in rocking chairs on a front porch. I thought that trying to dress modestly meant that I had to purchase and wear clothes that were dingy and frumpy and that I couldn't shop at stores with clothes that I would like or find pretty. I thought modesty would leave me as the one girl with the ugly dress at prom or that I'd always feel the clothes I had in my closet to wear on dates in my twenties were lackluster. Modesty felt more like a rule and an obligation than something I could embrace and choose freely. I wanted to live out the virtue of modesty, but I wanted to dress like a contemporary, modern young woman. So, I reshaped the way I saw modesty and began trying to dress as a *classy* woman.

When I think of classy women, I envision women like the singer Adele. To me, "classy" doesn't mean fancy or extravagant; it simply means honorable and illustrative of the respect I have for myself and my body. Adele is a woman who is always modestly dressed yet is dazzling and contemporary at the same time, even in casual clothes. She has single-handedly shown women everywhere that neither of the two lies being fed to us by the culture is true. Skin and power do not go hand in hand, and you don't have to show off your body to be noticed, liked, or even loved. She is consistently covered up yet fun and modern all at the same time—selling out stadiums in cities night after night, showing the world that she will happily share her gifts but not her body. She shows us that we don't have to bare it all to be a woman who can make an impact.

It is also important to remember that the way we dress does not give us more or less value. A woman who wears next to nothing does not have less value than a woman who is clothed in a beautiful, modest outfit. As I shared in our conversation on chastity, nothing you choose to do can diminish your value. Your value is *inherent*, which means it is permanent, and nothing can take it away. Dressing modestly is something we get to choose. When I choose clothes that cover my body in an appropriate way, I remind myself of my inherent dignity and worth and reflect it outwardly. When I dress with class, I show the world that I am a woman who respects herself. When I ask myself if an outfit outwardly reflects that I am a woman of strength and dignity, I remind myself that it is not my skin or my body where I should be deriving power or strength.

Authentic femininity is not weak. True femininity has an undeniable strength to it, and as women, our power and strength do not lie in how much skin we show but in our selflessness and our nurturing love. Our strength lies in our unique and feminine ability to sense when someone needs love or support. Our power lies in the ways our feminine hearts can nurture the world by the beauty we have to share from our hearts and minds. The amount of skin you show and the amount of power you have will never have any correlation with one another.

I talk to many young women who wonder if guys will still pay attention to them if they dress with their dignity and value in mind. If this is something you've felt or feared, I want you to know this: If guys were or are paying attention to you because you are showing a lot of skin, *those guys are not worth a second of your time or energy.* If it's showing a lot of skin that attracts a guy's attention, he is not the type of guy who is talking to you to get to know *you*; he is a boy, not a man, who is talking to you to get to know your body. He simply sees you as an object to be looked at, not a mind and heart to be known. Don't waste your time or emotions on guys who don't care about getting to know you for who you are rather than what you can do for them or for what your body looks like. Your personality, your intelligence, your quirks, and your beautiful heart are more than enough to attract a good guy who is worth spending time with.

Dressing with an awareness of *who you are* means that your personality can shine and that possible dates can be drawn to you for who you are rather than how much skin you are showing. Having this awareness of your inherent dignity means you can reflect that God-given dignity in everything you wear. Women who are kind, warm, selfless, and loving don't have to use their bodies to get attention. Instead, people are simply drawn to them because their hearts are radiant and rooted in the right place. You don't need to flaunt your body to be powerful, and you don't have to dress as a woman of dignity and grace just to follow rules. You can dress as a woman of dignity and grace because *you are one.*

"Strength and dignity are her clothing" (Proverbs 31:25a).

. . . .

TAKE ACTION

This can be a hard action. Are there clothes in your closet that don't reflect your inherent value and worth? Go through and get rid of them, remembering and reflecting on this verse from Proverbs 31.

FOURTEEN

Forgive and Forget

I love special life events that give me a reason to dress up and wear heels. Perhaps you know the type of event I'm talking about—the kind that requires the purchase of a special dress plus a hair and makeup appointment. Imagine with me that you are going to one of these events, and you've picked out a gorgeous dress and have been waiting for the night with great anticipation and excitement.

Now imagine yourself all dolled up and ready to hit the town, but you have to drag around a bag of bricks flung over your back all night. You have to take it in the car and to your dinner table. If there's dancing involved at this event, you have to carry it around on the dance floor while you display your best dance moves, and then you must lug it back home with you. It would be awful and difficult and would really prevent you from having a great time, wouldn't it?

This is the way I have always imagined what holding on to grudges, unforgiveness, and resentment looks like. It is completely synonymous with carrying around the burden of a bag of bricks, weighing you down constantly, keeping you from living a life of peace and freedom. Life is a beautiful journey that should be filled with freedom and joy, but when we are holding on to unforgiveness, clutching tightly to grudges and anger at others, it's as if we are lugging around a heavy bag while trying to live freely and joyfully.

Jesus taught frequently on the topic of forgiveness during his three years of ministry. In Matthew 18:21–22, he teaches that we should forgive seventy times seven times. One of the teachings that has resonated with me often in my life is the teaching Jesus gave through the parable of the unforgiving servant in Matthew 18:23–35. In that parable, a servant owes a great debt to his master and goes to him, begging that the debt be forgiven. The master shows the servant mercy and forgives his debt, but then the servant goes straight to someone who owes a debt to him and demands that the guy pay it back to him. The servant was shown great mercy, but mere moments later he is completely merciless when he has an opportunity to extend that same kind of mercy to another.

There have been so many times in my life when I have been the unmerciful servant. Thankfully, God's mercy is available to us all, in every moment of every day. Those who practice the Catholic faith are consistently given the opportunity to receive the limitless love and mercy of God through the sacrament of Reconciliation. Within this sacrament, no matter how big and extensive our sins, when we approach Christ with a heart of repentance and sorrow, he pours out his abundant mercy. We receive absolution that wipes our sins away, and we walk out of the confessional in the same way that the servant in the para-ble walked away from his master: all is forgiven and forgotten. Our wrongs are wiped clean, and Christ asks us to extend this same kind of loving mercy to the people in our lives. We say it every time we pray the Our Father: "Forgive us our trespasses, as we forgive those who trespass against us." In the parable of the unforgiving servant, Jesus highlights the utter hypocrisy of receiving God's mercy and then holding on to grudges and anger toward others, holding them accountable for their debts and never letting others forget what they owe.

This is so much easier said than done. The problem some-times lies in the fact that it can be really, really difficult to forgive. We all have people in our lives who have hurt us very badly, and the list of people who have hurt us will only grow as the years pass. Perhaps you're holding on to a grudge against a friend who betrayed your trust, purposely excluded you, or humil-iated you in some way. Maybe you were hurt in a breakup or had the horrible experience of being cheated on by a boyfriend. Maybe there's a girl in your school or your dorm who started an ugly rumor about you, or you were the victim of gossip. Perhaps you're holding on to anger toward that teacher or professor who gave you a bad grade and wouldn't give you an opportunity to make it up in some way. Or maybe you have feelings of deep resentment toward one of your parents for something they did or failed to do for you.

In our humanity, it can often feel nearly impossible to for-give when people hurt us in little ways or in very deep ways, because forgiveness feels contrary to what our minds tell us is fair after someone has caused us pain. No matter how badly we have been hurt, it is crucial to remember that *forgiveness is not a feeling*. Forgiveness will never be a feeling. Forgiveness is a deliberate choice you and I get to make when people have hurt, wronged, or betrayed us, and it is often a choice that does not come naturally when people have caused us deep hurt. Revenge and anger come naturally. We want to get back at those people; we want to make them pay for what they have done—we are the unmerciful servant.

While we may *feel* as though holding on to grudges and unforgiveness is fair and just, in reality, carrying around unforgiveness actually compounds on the hurt that was done to us. When we carry around this burden, we are allowing that person to continue to hurt us. Most likely, that person isn't putting another ounce of energy into thinking about the situation, but sometimes we let it consume us and distress us for long periods of time. We aren't hurting that person by holding on to a grudge. We are hurting ourselves. We are carrying around a bag of bricks through life when we have the ability to let it go. Sometimes, however, we can't let it go by ourselves. We have to ask God for the strength to do so.

God is always willing to aid us in making the deliberate choice to forgive. Jesus can fortify us with the strength to make good choices for ourselves—and when asked for help, he can certainly help open your capacity for forgiveness in your heart. Jesus had the capacity in his heart to forgive those who killed him, even while he was on the Cross (see Luke 23:34). When we allow Christ to help us let go and forgive, we also allow him to mend those broken and wounded places within us and restore our faith and trust in others. We allow him to heal our hearts, which is something we cannot do for ourselves.

My question for you is this: Are you holding on to unforgiveness or grudges in your heart toward one person or a group of people? Are you allowing the hurt that they did to you to continue to affect your everyday life? Are you lugging that bag of bricks around in your nice gown and heels at an imaginary event? No matter how beautiful you look at that event, no matter how expensive your dress is, no matter how perfectly your curls came out, you can't possibly have a good time if you're trying to dance or talk to people while carrying this bag around. Today I encourage you to work toward letting those grudges or resentments go. Pray fervently about it. Talk to God about it, and tell him how you feel. Ask him for the strength to make the deliberate choice to forgive and to lay your hurts down before him so that he can heal you, restore your heart, and help you move forward in freedom.

· ·

TAKE ACTION

Is there someone you need to forgive? Is there a grudge you have been holding on to for a little or a long time? Ask God for the grace today to choose to forgive that person, whether in your heart, to his or her face, or in a message to that person—whatever would be most freeing for you.

FIFTEEN

Keep Calm and Follow God

It is the vocation of every Christian, not only of a few elect, to belong to God in love's free surrender and to serve him. Whether man or woman, whether consecrated or not, each one is called to the imitation of Christ.

—Edith Stein (St. Teresa Benedicta
of the Cross), *Essays on Woman*

Discovering one's vocation is one of the most common topics young women want to discuss with me. They ask me, "How did you figure out what your vocation was? How will I know what mine is? What if I choose the wrong one? What if the vocation God has in mind for me will make me totally unhappy?" The women who ask me these questions often express feelings of anxiety and frustration over the quest to find the path God wants them to take. But God did not design vocational discernment to be a journey of exasperation and unease.

One of my favorite quotes about the topic of vocations is from St. Teresa of Calcutta, who said, "Many people mistake our work for our vocation. Our vocation is the love of Jesus." Before we talk about marriage, single life, or consecrated life, we must recognize that the first and overarching call of our lives is to be the hands and feet of Jesus Christ in the world (see 1 Corinthians 12:27). We are called to love those around us as Christ does—to pour the love of Christ into their hearts and to be light in their life. That is a beautiful responsibility and deeply radical calling in and of itself.

Beyond this foundational vocation is what I call our "Big V" vocation. This is a person's individual calling from God to marriage, to the religious life, or to the single life.

As you discern your specific vocational calling in your life, there are two absolute truths that I want you to understand. The first is that God knows you, and knows your heart (see Jeremiah 1:5). The second is that the plans he has for your life are *good* (see Jeremiah 29:11). He is not out to torture you and force you into a vocation that will make you depressed, unhappy, and lifeless. Does this mean that your vocation will be easy and free of any trial or suffering? Absolutely not. But he has willed a vocation for you that will make you feel alive and deeply fulfilled because he knows your heart intimately enough to know what path will truly make you come alive.

Discerning our vocation firstly requires an openness to God and his will for us. Figuring out your vocation is not like solving a puzzle, getting to the end of a maze, or crossing a finish line. God did not intend it to be an anxiety-ridden search for answers. Figuring out your vocation by way of careful discernment should be a process where you learn more about the heart of God as well as your own heart and, in doing that, grow in trust of the Father and his will for you. It should be a process of further exploration of who you are and who God created you to be.

As I sought out the path God planned for me in my vocation, sometimes I convinced myself that God must be playing games with me, that he was purposefully being mysterious for no reason at all. In my discernment of my vocation, I experienced a few panic attacks derived from my fear of God's will for my life. Through the love and care of trusted people, I came to learn that God does not tease us and say, "I want you to be married!" or "You are called to religious life!" and then mysteriously disappear, leaving us alone to figure out how to find our way to that path. St. Paul says very clearly in 1 Corinthians 14:33 (RSVCE) that "God is not a God of confusion but of peace." In John 10, when Jesus calls himself the loving shepherd, he is revealing that it is in his nature to guide us, not drive us in fear, anguish, or confusion. He wants to guide you lovingly to his call for your life. He doesn't point to a certain vocation and say, "Figure out how to get there." He lovingly reveals a vocation and quietly says, "Let me guide you there."

While all women may feel that attraction to motherhood in our humanity, God puts a glimmer in the hearts of some women for religious life if they are supposed to embrace God's call for them in that specific way. It brings them joy. In her *Essays on*

Woman, Edith Stein said in regard to religious life that "whoever sees this way open before her will yearn for no other way." Through prayer, the thought and beauty of the life God wills for you should bring you serenity, calm, and delight, even in the midst of the sometimes-painful surrender of letting go of your own plans and conforming your will to God's.

God alone will call you to what he wills for you, but the process of discernment of your vocation can be helped by the counsel of a good spiritual director. Spiritual direction is a practice through which you can meet regularly with someone, either a religious or layperson, who can help guide you in your spiritual life and help you see where God is moving in your heart and in your life. This person can assist you in seeing what God is revealing to you about the vocation that will bring you the most fulfillment and that will allow him to use your gifts to their fullest capacity in a world in desperate need of his love.

As you walk carefully with Jesus, he will, in love, reveal the vocation to which he is calling you. As you walk with him, do not obsess. Do not overthink. Do not panic. Breathe in and, as St. Teresa of Calcutta said, "Bloom where you are planted." There are people around you in this very season of your life who need the love of Christ today—do not miss the opportunity to love those people because you are obsessing about the future. Focus now on fulfilling that first vocation to be Christ to everyone around you and simply to be open to where God wants to lead you forward. God is not asking you to worry endlessly about your vocation or what you will do with all your days. God has you right where he wants you in this very moment, and as you walk faithfully with him, he will guide you along with his glorious and loving hand. He will show you the way in peace and in love.

Pope emeritus Benedict XVI gave a beautiful homily on the day he began his ministry as pope. It has been a theme of my life in Christ and has helped me especially on my journey to my vocation of marriage. Perhaps it can bring you solace and courage, too:

> Are we not perhaps all afraid in some way? If we let Christ enter fully into our lives, if we open ourselves totally to him, are we not afraid that he might take something away from us? Are we not perhaps afraid to give up something significant, something unique, something that makes life so beautiful? Do we not then risk ending up diminished and deprived of our freedom? . . . No! If we let Christ into our lives, we lose nothing, nothing, absolutely nothing of what makes life free, beautiful and great. No! Only in this friendship are the doors of life opened wide. Only in this friendship is the great potential of human existence truly revealed. Only in this friendship do we experience beauty and liberation. And so, today, with great strength and great conviction, on the basis of long personal experience of life, I say to you, dear young people: Do not be afraid of Christ! He takes nothing away, and he gives you everything. When we give ourselves to him, we receive a hundredfold in return. Yes, open, open wide the doors to Christ— and you will find true life. Amen.

. . . .

TAKE ACTION

Don't feel pressure to *do* anything about your vocation right now. The best action you can take is to continue to develop a strong prayer life so that communication between you and God is a regular thing. If you feel God calling you at any point to go on a discernment retreat, do so. When the time comes to choose a path in life, you'll be ready to listen to him and to act.

SIXTEEN

Exercise Your "No" Muscle

Have you ever spent time with a three-year-old? It is around this time that we, as humans, really begin to develop our wills. Three-year-olds start to realize that they can decide, quite firmly, what they do and do not want to do. They can be extremely stubborn once they realize that they can either decide to listen to their mother's commands or say no. Most mothers would probably tell you that their toddler's favorite word is "no." No naps. No broccoli. No sharing. No bath. This is not a flimsy no either. It is a no with often strong volume and gumption.

That said, while our "no" muscle is quite well developed as toddlers, our ability to say the word seems to wear away over time. When our human desire to be accepted and liked by our peers begins to come into play, we may grow less and less comfortable with using this word.

In middle and high school and throughout college, a more palpable desire to be accepted by others begins to form in our hearts. It is a natural inclination in every human being to want to be accepted by the people around us. This desire is only compounded by the reality that our world puts incredibly large stock in popularity, approval, affirmation, and the opinions of others. Nobody wants to be made the fool, to be an outcast, or to be alone. During our teenage years, societal pressure and temptation come into play, and we almost begin to forget how to say that word we were so attached to when we were very small. Peer pressure is such a mighty force that sometimes we begin to say yes to things that we would rather decline—parties, gossip, drinking, drugs, cheating, teasing, sending inappropriate photos or messages, excluding other people, and more. When someone stands in front of us and asks us if we want to participate in one of those things, it can be very difficult to channel the three-year-old within and remember how to say no. Our desire for acceptance can cause us to consent to things we know in our hearts we don't really want to do. Our fear of being made fun of or being rejected or being labeled "uncool" can begin to sway our decisions.

In the face of every pressure that comes along with being a young woman, it is imperative to remember that each of us has the power to say yes *and* no in every facet of our lives. No one can make decisions for us, and we each must live in the consequences of our decisions, both our positive ones and our negative ones. Saying no to things can be very challenging, as is everything else we've been talking about in this book! It often requires incredible boldness to say no when all we may hear is a little voice in our head shouting, "Just say yes! You'll look foolish if you don't! They'll laugh at you if you say no! They won't like you if you decline the invitation and walk away!" You have to dig deep and bravely muster up that resilient spirit you were so comfortable exhibiting when you were three.

Pursuing virtue involves frequently saying no to the things of the world, even though the world often declares that the people who say no to what is cool, accepted, or normal are Goody Two-Shoes who can't have fun or who are bringing everyone else down. What our culture will not tell you is that this no that we must say to the temptations of the world is actually a yes to a life of freedom and fulfillment. Our ability to say no can free us from a life of guilt and shame. When we master saying no to things we do not want to be a part of or that we know are not good for us, we say yes to the life that God is calling us to live.

The word "no" has the power to set you free. It has the power to cultivate peace in your life and has the ability to bring you continually closer to Christ. Remember this: Bravely making good choices will always set you free.

The power to use this word rests in your hands. It takes practice; saying no to one thing makes it easier to say no to the next thing. While I attended school at Arizona State, I had to use the word "no" a lot in trying to live a life of faith. I constantly had to tell people that I did not want to go to the party they invited me to, that I did not want to drink with them before football games. I had to say no when guys gave me attention and asked me to come back to their dorm. I didn't say it loudly like a three-year-old saying no to a nap, but I had to be polite yet firm about it.

Was every no challenging in its own way? Absolutely. I loathed being made fun of. I struggled a lot with the fact that people labeled me as judgmental even though I was simply and quietly trying to pave my own way. I wanted to fit in and feel as though I belonged and was accepted by my peers. I had moments when it was very uncomfortable not to be able to do what everyone else seemed to be doing. As I have already shared, I felt very lonely at times, but I had to live with the constant awareness that a yes to a situation that I knew would lead me to temptation and peer pressure always had the potential to have serious negative consequences in my life. If we are living in a way that reflects who we are and who God created us to be, we must go forward with humility, bravely making hard decisions again and again.

Every no I had the courage to say was necessary to keep me on the road I knew I wanted to be on. I forged ahead with the hope that it would be worthwhile to live a life that was different. Now that I have made it through middle school, high school, and college, I can tell you with assurance that it was worthwhile. Every no to the pressures of the world was a step toward the life that I knew, deep down in my heart, would fulfill me. I believe wholeheartedly that this word can have the same function for you.

If you are striving to pursue virtue and trying your very best to make positive decisions that uplift you rather than leave you with regret, bring out that inner three-year-old. Do not be afraid to stand up for yourself and bravely choose the road you know you need to be on. Exercise that "no" muscle when you know deep down in your heart that you need to. It is a key to freedom from the chains of sin and shame. It is a key to true happiness. It is a key that will continually help you live as the woman God created you to be.

• •

TAKE ACTION

Has there ever been a moment in your life when you wanted to say no but didn't? Reflect on that moment.

- What can you learn from it?
- What kept you from saying what you really wanted to say?
- How can you set yourself up to be able to say what you know you need to the next time a situation like that arises in your life?

SEVENTEEN

Love Your Body

Throughout our entire lives, the media has presented us with a cookie-cutter image of the "perfect body." This body ideal has been shown to us in thousands of images, advertisements, and marketing campaigns. The culture consistently presents the idea that toned abs, a thigh gap, and pronounced collarbones are what make a body beautiful. We don't see cellulite in advertisements. I have never seen a woman on a billboard or the cover of a magazine who has stretch marks like the ones I see on my own legs in the mirror. We don't often see women of different shapes and sizes wearing the clothes a store is selling. The world has decided that those things should be hidden, covered up, because they are unattractive. They are unsightly. They are *ugly*.

Combine this message with the pressure to eat the latest fad diet in order to lose weight: gluten-free, dairy-free, Paleo, vegan—you name it! We're constantly consuming the idea that we are not good enough. It's not just attributes of our bodies that are ugly—*we* are ugly.

When we believe that any part of us is ugly, we feel compelled to hide or change that part of ourselves. We often begin to push ourselves, trying to stuff ourselves into this mold, this cookie-cutter shape that the world tells us is the standard of beauty, a shape we weren't designed to fit into in the first place. What I have found is that this pushing and forcing and trying to fit into an often-unattainable mold leads to exhaustion, sadness, and deep struggle. Exercise becomes the avenue by which we can fix the parts of ourselves that we deem ugly. It becomes a tool for crafting the perfect figure—a means to put curves on what people have told you is a boyish body or to slim down to see perfectly defined muscles. Food becomes the enemy, something that we obsess over and allow to dictate and control so much of our days and our energy. But exercise is actually something we should do to take care of our bodies, and food exists to nourish us!

As I have already shared with you in this book, God dwells within you and me. We are temples of the Holy Spirit, with God alive in us, but often we do not act as though this is the case. So often we look in the mirror at our bodies and see all the things we wish we could change, instead of thinking, *God dwells within me.* So often we compare our looks to those of another woman and think, *If only I could look like that, then I would finally be happy with myself.* I have done this hundreds of times.

The beauty of God's creation is that not a single human being has been repeated. This incredible reality means that you weren't meant to look like the girls from your school, on your Instagram feed, in your friend group, or on magazine covers. You were meant to look like you. Your body is a beautiful creation. You are unrepeatable. There is no one in the world who will ever be you. On top of *that*, you come from a completely unique ancestral line, with a heritage that is different from that of the women sitting to your right or left. This is what the cookie-cutter concept forgets.

Our bodies are built differently based on where our ancestors came from. Some of us have big hips, and some of us don't. We carry our weight in different places. Some heritages pass on broad shoulders. Some of us find it difficult to gain weight or achieve the curves we wish we had. Some of us could never achieve a thigh gap no matter how hard we tried. These are things no advertisement will tell you. These are things we don't remember when we are looking at another woman's seemingly "better" body displayed on her social media or at the beach, but they are the things we need to keep at the forefront of our minds. These truths help us celebrate the distinct beauty we each possess.

For a long time, I listened to the lies about what makes a beautiful body. I struggled for years with my body image and wishing I could change where I carry my weight—and it is a struggle that did not end overnight. I have gone through much healing from harmful thoughts and behavior patterns related to my body image. In the past, I would often think about my body with worry and anxiety for hours in a day. My body stores its fat on my sides, and the world was telling me this shouldn't be, that I should work to get it off. Muffin tops aren't attractive; they are ugly—they need to be changed and fixed, the world says. I exercised constantly in order to change my body, not to keep it well. It was exhausting. When I was introduced to the idea of taking care of my body because I love it, I knew deeply I had to shift my focus.

I knew without a doubt that I had to shift my efforts from exercising to try to fit into a mold to exercising and eating well in order to be happy, healthy, and strong. The first scenario was leading me on a road of perpetual exhaustion and self-hatred. I knew the second scenario was the true way to peace within me and the path to loving the body God gave me. I had a deep and powerful realization that tirelessly trying to fit into a mold isn't what God made me for.

So I began to pray fervently: "Lord, help me to love my body. Help me to love my temple. Help me to embrace the uniqueness of my body. Help me to see food as nourishment rather than a thing to be calculated or controlled. Help me to recognize that my body is unique and that my stretch marks aren't ugly. They are normal for some women, and they are a part of me." I asked the Lord to heal my heart and the poor self-image I had developed because of the images that I had seen throughout my life—the images that had caused me to believe that my body was not beautiful and should be changed. Slowly but surely, he did. He is faithful.

As I began to love my body intentionally, I had to completely flip my attitude about eating and exercise. I started to despise it when my Zumba instructor would waltz in after a holiday weekend and jokingly shout, "Time to work off all that pie you ladies ate over the weekend!" I had to remember that when I exercise, I am not working off pie! I would step back and reframe my thinking to understand and remember that eating does not add stuff to my body that I have to take off by exercising. When I exercise, I am loving my body and engaging in something that makes me healthier, both physically and mentally. I am taking care of my body, and I am treating it as I am supposed to.

Exercise does not have to mean hitting the gym every day—sometimes my gym is full of smelly men, and some days I'm just not in the mood to be smelling men while I exercise. Taking care of our bodies can and should be an enjoyable thing. Experiment with different kinds of exercise, and find what you love. Get outside and go on walks, lift some weights, or take a dance class. Get some friends together for an afternoon hike, or join a recreational soccer league. Sign up for a spin class. Perhaps you can commit to taking one thirty-minute walk or run every day when you get home from school or work. There are so many ways to get your body moving! It can also be helpful to find a friend who wants to take care of her body right alongside you so that you can do it together.

Building strength in your muscles and in your body can increase your confidence in ways you never anticipated. Getting moving and working up a sweat regularly is a wonderful habit to form and can make a powerful difference in your life and your health. The important piece is remembering to exercise because you love your body, not because you hate it.

Treating food as nourishment and taking care of our bodies through healthy eating is just as important as exercising! It's often said that "the way to a man's heart is through his stomach." This saying can definitely apply to women as well. Have you ever seen a group of women react when another woman walks up with a box of cupcakes? The excitement is real. One time at an event, two girls gave me a box of a dozen gourmet doughnuts they had picked out just for me, and I nearly got teary-eyed with joy! I, however, have had to find a balance with eating things that make me feel happy and healthy and things that aren't necessarily as nutritious—such as the delicious menu at In-N-Out Burger in California (one of my favorite places ever).

Mindful eating is a crucial component to loving our bodies because nutritious foods fuel our bodies properly. They give us energy to get through the school day, work day, and even our exercise. Pancakes, chips, quesadillas, pizza, ice cream—those things are great, but if I am consuming them too regularly, they don't fuel my body properly. Fresh fruits, vegetables, salads, good proteins, and meats—these kinds of foods give my body the energy and sustenance it wants and needs.

An important aspect of implementing mindful eating in my life was learning how to cook. I did not really enjoy cooking when I first began doing it (and I was definitely *not* great at it), but I found that the more I practiced, the more my food and techniques improved, and the more I enjoyed it (and the effect it had on my bank account when I wasn't constantly eating out!). In the past, if women didn't have a cookbook, there was nowhere for them to get recipes. Our access to the Internet today gives us the ability to find an innumerable number of recipes to make foods for every taste. If you're clueless in the kitchen, do some research online for healthy, delicious meal options. If you have a friend or family member who can cook healthy meals, have them over to your house to give you some great cooking tips or to share with you some of their favorite recipes. Eating healthy doesn't have to be a burden. If approached in the right way, it can be really fun and can contribute positively to your overall physical and mental health at the same time.

We are each individually responsible for choosing to take good care of our bodies in our eating and exercise habits, but it takes conscious and purposeful effort. Dig in and put in that effort to form habits that will contribute to the wellness of your body, mind, and spirit. Make the conscious and purposeful choice to love yourself by working up a sweat and by eating good things. When we do this, we become more of who God created us to be as women: happy, healthy, and strong.

. . . .

TAKE ACTION

Reflect on your eating and exercise habits.

- Are you taking good care of your body or choosing not to?
- Where can you make changes in your life to love your body more?

Write those changes down—and if you want to go a step further, find an accountability partner to help you make healthier choices and perhaps get an exercise plan going!

EIGHTEEN

Ignore the Haters

In November 2007, my friend Eric asked to meet in the cafeteria in the Manzanita Hall dorm at ASU. I had no idea what he wanted to talk about, but the conversation that transpired over that dinner was completely unexpected and caught me off guard in a way I had never experienced.

Eric and I were part of a small living-learning community of journalism students. We shared a specially designated dorm with other students majoring in interior or architectural design. There were about 150 people in our building, and sometimes it felt like an episode of a bad reality television show. Everyone knew who everyone else was, gossip reigned supreme, and stories traveled quickly through the halls. I made friends with the other journalism students, and we spent a lot of time together. Over our dinner, however, Eric told me that he wanted to make me aware of everything that had been transpiring behind my back for the past few months at our dorm. I was stunned as he started talking.

"Everyone talks about you all the time," he said. "They say that you're stuck-up and judgmental. They say you don't really want friends, that you just want attention. Everyone's speculating about why you don't bring guys back to your room like the other girls do. Emily, everyone thinks you're fake, and nobody likes having you around."

"Are there specific people who are saying this?" I asked.

"*Everyone*," he said.

His words felt like a hard, heavy, brutal slap across the face. I was in disbelief. I had been vulnerable with these people. I had been open and shared things about my life with them, and this is what was happening all along? The conversation becomes a bit blurry after that. I remember crying, leaving, and walking home, wondering where I could have gone wrong.

"Nobody likes having you around." Among all the words spoken over that dinner, this is the lie that was imprinted onto my heart at that table in the cafeteria. I can't explain exactly why it affected me so deeply, but this sentence was etched into me like a chisel to marble, and it became a lie that would resonate in my heart and head for a very long time. My "friendships" with those people were over, and I felt totally alone, betrayed, and rejected. In the weeks after, I attempted to reach out to another group of people in my dorm, but they made it very clear that they had heard about me and didn't want me around either. The biggest mistake that I made as a result of that conversation was to allow the opinions of these people to dictate my behavior for a long time.

For many years after that conversation, I felt deep anxiety in social situations, wondering if I was doing things correctly or if my actions were causing people to think those same things that everyone in my dorm said about me. I was afraid to get close to anyone, terrified that I would be betrayed again, so I didn't allow anyone to get close to me. This made genuine friendship nearly impossible. Friendship requires that two people share their hearts and have a mutual openness with one another, and I was too afraid to let that happen, so I kept everyone at arm's length with the belief that if they didn't get to know me, then they couldn't find things that they didn't like about me.

When I got home from social gatherings, I would worry endlessly about every word that I said that night, terrified that I said the wrong thing or said something that made me look like a fool or made people think, "Boy, it would be better if this girl wasn't here." I couldn't enjoy spending time in social situations. It was awful, but I continued to let the opinions of these people dictate my thoughts and behavior for years. It is heartbreaking for me to think about now, but the truth is that I lived and acted from a place where I believed the opinions of others rather than the truth of who God says I am.

While I kept everyone at a distance, I was completely miserable. I lived in fear and trembling about people saying nasty things. I desperately wanted close friendships, but I feared betrayal so deeply. In my misery, I came to a place where I realized that I had to let God sand out this etching that I had let those people carve into my heart. If I was ever going to enjoy my life, if I was ever going to have good, true friendships, if I was ever going to be able to hang out with my friends without replaying everything I said in my head, I had to put in the work to defeat these lies I had believed for so long. I had to seek healing. I had to seek Christ, the Healer.

How does one go about doing this? Lies can only be defeated by truth, and I had to go back to the root of who God says I am. I had to remember my identity as daughter. I had to go to God and ask for healing from the lies I had believed for so long. In learning to defeat the lies, my constant prayer became: "God, show me who I am." When I spoke these words and allowed myself to be open to God's response, I had to accept his response as truth. There is a scripture verse that has meant a lot to me in seeking healing from these insecurities, from the book of Zephaniah: "The LORD, your God, is in your midst, a warrior who gives victory; he will rejoice over you with gladness, he will renew you in his love; he will exult over you with loud singing as on a day of festival" (Zephaniah 3:17–18).

Throughout my process of healing, I have come to see that God heals people in different ways. Jesus did many instantaneous healings in the gospels, whether he was healing lepers (see Matthew 8:1–4), raising a little girl from the dead (see Matthew 9:18–26), or helping the blind see (Mark 10:46–52). As much as I wanted Jesus to heal my painful insecurities in one miraculous flash of his power, he didn't. Instead, Jesus has taken me on a journey of healing. I have continually opened my heart to the healing of God who delights greatly in me, and who wants to spend time with me. I came to a place over and over again where I had to accept the reality that God has placed people in my life who love me for who I am and who genuinely enjoy having me around. Accepting this to be true was extremely difficult, as Eric's words—"nobody likes having you around"—would replay again and again in my heart, often out of the blue. I had to learn to accept the love of others and offer my hand in friendship to others, even though the risk of rejection always remains.

The healing I have experienced from these lies was not instantaneous. It has been a process and a journey, and what I have come to find is that God has healed this lie in my heart *one letter at a time*. With his gentle and loving hand, through different experiences of his love in prayer and through others, God slowly sanded out this lie that was etched onto my heart, one small memory and moment at a time. With first the "N," and then the "o," he continued to heal me until I could see that people did want me around, that I am loved for who I am, that I could be healed from my insecurity, and that the truth that God says about who I am is the truth that stands forever. I am profoundly grateful for the healing God has done in my heart and in my life.

None of us will be exempt from having untrue or unkind things said about us, to our faces or behind our backs. You may know this all too well. Perhaps you have been bullied by one or many people. Maybe you have been the target of an ugly rumor or have been misjudged by friends or by an entire community. It hurts very badly. It is an inescapable reality that people will say all different kinds of things about you throughout your life—nice things, mean things, beautiful things, and false things.

But as we discussed earlier in this book, in the chapter about extending kindness toward other women, it is insecure people

who utter ugly and hateful words about others. Confident people never put other people down. They don't have the time or
room in their life for it. Insecurity (perhaps mixed with some
boredom) was the very thing that compelled these "friends" in
my dorm to speak so frequently and unkindly about who I am. I
wish I had been able to see at the time that all the unkind words
were flowing directly from their own insecurities, but I did not
know that then. But I can tell you that now. I want you to know
that the people who put you down in your life—the people who
say that you are good-for-nothing, the people who feel any need
to comment on your body shape, your looks, or your capabilities—those people are telling you by their words that they are
insecure, and they're taking their insecurities out on you. You
must combat the lies by going to God, by falling at the feet of a
Father who only and always speaks good things about you.

The truth God speaks about you and over you is the only
truth that will stand amid all the noise. I want you to hear me
loud and clear on this, because I don't want you to spend years
like I did believing the lies others have spoken of you. In those
moments when you are swimming in confusion about who you
are—torn between who God says you are and all the things that
everyone else has said about you and who everyone else may
expect you to be—I want you to tuck that simple and profound
prayer close to your heart for those moments: "God, show me
who I am."

This prayer has been a crux of my faith and my healing from
the wounds I carried from the mean words of these people,
and I hope it will be helpful for you, too. But remember that

it requires a listening and attentiveness to what God has to say after you pray it. Sometimes God speaks in words, and sometimes he speaks in images. Sometimes his response takes time. Most recently, as I prayed this prayer, I had a memory from my childhood of a time when my dad would carry my sisters and me around on his legs as we held on screaming with delight, arms and legs wrapped tightly around his leg. God was stirring within me the knowledge that I am a thoroughly and truly precious daughter, deeply loved by both my earthly father and my heavenly Father. God delights in telling you who you are. He wants to shatter the lies that may have impacted your confidence and your self-image. He wants to speak truth to your heart—but in order to be able to hear him you must ask and be open.

Hear me clearly when I tell you this, my sister. As I tell you this, I tell it to myself once again:

> You are loved, worthy, and set apart for God's great purpose for your life. He delights in who you are and created you to take part in his divine plan for the world. You are not a burden. There are people who enjoy your company, who love you for who you are, and who genuinely want you around. Do not let what anyone else says or thinks *ever* convince you otherwise.

. . . .

TAKE ACTION

If you have ever believed the lies or wrongful opinions others have spoken of you, take some time to say this out loud:

> I am loved, worthy, and set apart for God's great purpose for my life. He delights in who I am and created me to take part in his divine plan for the world. I am not a burden. There are people who enjoy my company, who love me for who I am, and who genuinely want me around. I will not let what anyone else says or thinks *ever* convince me otherwise.

Say this as many times, or on as many days, as you need to in order to start believing it.

NINETEEN

Radiate with Light

I was standing in a room at a youth conference in Amarillo, Texas, when a kind woman asked me to share my "conversion story" with her. I have been asked to do this a few times since, and I've wondered why people ask and presume that everyone has such a story.

When I was a campus minister at a high school, I had many young women who wanted to lead retreats, but who shared that they didn't feel qualified because they did not have some earth-shaking testimony or story of great conversion filled with dramatic details and exciting fireworks. I have continued to hear this from young people: "Can I still lead retreats or ministries or give talks if I don't have a story?" Listeners in an audience surely love good stories and eventful tales, but these young women did not feel that they were even qualified to lead if they had not wandered far away, returned to God, and could give a great talk based on this testimony.

My conversion story . . . is that I do not have one. Has my journey been perfect? No, certainly not, but I do not have a dramatic story of finding my faith or coming back to my faith. However, the fact that I do not have the kind of "conversion" story that people would consider engaging and exciting does not mean I do not have an important testimony to share with the people I encounter.

Perhaps you find yourself like me or some of the young women who expressed this concern to me: You don't have a history of falling far away from God, or you've never had a season when you stopped going to church for a certain number of months or years and came back to him in a moment of great freedom or fanfare. It is certainly a beautiful thing if you have a powerful testimony of conversion—if it is your story. But you can bravely share your journey of faith no matter how many twists and turns it has or has not taken.

Take Saul, for example. He was blinded by God's light in a moment of monumental conversion (see Acts 9:3–4). The prodigal son erred greatly in his ways and came running home to his father after having squandered everything and fallen into a life of sin (see Luke 15:11–32). However, you do not need this type of story to share the beauty of redemption and the Gospel. You do not need a testimony full of fireworks to be a great leader. Everyone's story is powerful. Everyone's story of faith matters and reflects the goodness of God. And the beauty of Christ's followers is that each of our stories is different. Each story of conversion, each story of faithfulness, each story of God's great forgiveness—they are as unique as every one of us. They are all stories worth telling. We simply get to decide whether or not we will boldly testify to our friends, family, neighbors, classmates, or strangers about the beautiful and constant power and mercy of our good God.

St. Peter tells us to "always be ready to make your defense to anyone who demands from you an accounting for the hope that is in you" (1 Peter 3:15). This means that, no matter what our testimony is, no matter the road by which we came to know and love Jesus Christ, we should always be ready to share it. This can be a scary thought! Be brave. We should always be equipped and prepared to share about our faith with anyone who may notice that we live differently, or anyone who asks, "Do you believe in God?" or "Why do you go to church?"

As I have already shared, sometimes it can be difficult to discuss our faith openly. It can be uncomfortable because talking about Jesus in today's world is entirely unconventional and uncommon. So how do we do that? We first have to be unafraid to tell people that we do go to church or that we are Christian or Catholic. It sounds quite simple, but it can be difficult even to say those things—that we have to make sure we get to church on Sunday or that we care a lot about our faith—whether to a stranger, a new friend, or a date. It is often a reality that we can skate around if we want to, for fear that others will think we are "weird" or "different."

A few years ago I was on a flight to an event and shared with a woman sitting next to me about my faith, and she was shocked as I told her about how much I love having a relationship with Jesus and that it is the most important aspect of my life. She told me she didn't even know there were people in America who were still Catholic. (I was tempted to ask her if she lived under a rock, but I refrained!) I was so glad that I had shared my faith with her just so she could see a living, breathing, young woman who loves Jesus.

Matthew 5 proclaims the truth that, as Christians, we are the light of the world, and *we cannot hide our light.* There have been so many moments when I have hidden the light of my faith— such as in a conversation with a new friend or stranger, brushing it off as though I didn't care about my faith because I was worried about what that person would think or the questions he or she would have for me. I have found time and time again that it is easier to hide my faith than it is to share it, just as easy as it is to forget my identity as daughter of God rather than live it. I am not proud of those moments in my life, because I passed up an opportunity to tell someone about the Jesus whose love has changed my life and whose love could also change theirs. I was too nervous or worried, and there have even been occasions when I just didn't feel like it.

Every time I fail to share my testimony of faith or speak about Jesus Christ with someone, I am preventing the light of God from shining forth from my heart. Perhaps Jesus wants to illuminate that person's heart through my heart that's on fire for him, but I allow my fear to be an obstacle.

Telling others about what Christ has done in your life invites them to explore the possibility that he can do the very same thing for them. Sharing your testimony reflects the light of Christ directly into the life of the person you are sharing with. You may even be the first person who ever tells them about Jesus Christ. After all, everyone in the world who believes in Jesus has a person who first told them about him. Sharing your faith invites people to an openness to the possibility that—if they are not already—they too can live for something bigger than themselves, can find a peace and joy that the world will never be able to offer, and can be redeemed and restored by the love and mercy of a loving Father.

If you are going to be comfortable, confident, and courageous in sharing about your faith, it is important to step back and dedicate some time to really thinking about what you would say to someone who asked you, "Why should I believe in God?" Maybe you feel that if someone asked you that question, you'd clam up and start sweating. Each and every person of faith should have an answer to this question and be able to share that answer readily. If you have never given thought to what your answer to this question is, explore it. Pray about it. Write some things down. If you feel that you wouldn't be able to give a good explanation of your faith beyond "Well . . . because," then look for opportunities to learn about your faith! Talk to people who know a lot about your faith, and ask them questions or read books that will help you explain your beliefs well. There are countless resources at our disposal designed and created to help us learn and grow in our faith, and knowledge and understanding can boost our ability to exercise bravery and equip us to shine brightly.

When Jesus sends out the twelve disciples in Matthew 10, he is sending us out, too. The disciples are no longer alive here on earth, so we are to carry the message of Jesus Christ to the world in the same way they did. That doesn't mean standing on platforms in the middle of your city giving big talks. It means telling the person in front of you about the God who saves. When I meet God on the day that I die, I hope that I can echo the words of Psalm 40:10: "I have not hidden your saving help within my heart, I have spoken of your faithfulness and your salvation; I have not concealed your steadfast love and your faithfulness from the great congregation." Hiding your testimony and the reason for your hope does a great disservice to the people whose lives could be changed by your hope. Your testimony, whatever it may be, is filled with the light and love of God. Do not be afraid to share it with the world.

"You are the light of the world. A city built on a hill cannot be hid. No one after lighting a lamp puts it under the bushel basket, but on the lampstand, and it gives light to all in the house. In the same way, let your light shine before others, so that they may see your good works and give glory to your Father in heaven" (Matthew 5:14–16).

. . . .

TAKE ACTION

Think about what your answer would be if someone walked up to you and asked, "Why should I believe in

God?" What would you share with that person? Write it down, and unpack your response.

TWENTY

Live It Up

A few years ago I spoke at a college conference in Virginia, and after my talk two young women came up to me with a serious concern. They were burdened by the idea that if they love God and dedicate themselves to living a life of faith, they have to be praying in a church all the time. They expressed that they feel guilty enjoying their lives, hanging out with their friends, and even playing sports.

I am asked these questions frequently: "If I follow God, can I live life as a young person who likes to have fun and hang out with my friends? Do I have to give up my phone, TV, and other fun activities and just pray all the time?" The answer is, yes, you can enjoy your life, and, no, you don't have to give everything up and pray in a chapel all the time!

My wonderful grandmother taught me to enjoy life in a very reflective way by the way she lived out the well-known saying "Stop and smell the roses." Nana soaked up moments with a profound and incalculable enjoyment and presence. Whether it was a song she was listening to, a book she was reading, or a person she was having a conversation with—she was entirely present to it and wrung out every last bit of delight in it that she possibly could. In the midst of it all, she knew that in every ounce of enjoyment, she was experiencing the heart of God.

God created laughter. He gave us bodies that we can dance in. He created babies and bunnies and the oceans and mountains and so many other cute and beautiful things. I love bunnies more than I could possibly tell you—they bring me so much joy! Do you think he made all the beauty of the world for us to dismiss it and do everything we can not to enjoy it? No! He wants us to enjoy life! He also invites us to be *in* the world but not *of* the world (see John 17:14–15).

Pope Francis said in a 2014 message on the five-hundredth anniversary of the birth of St. Teresa of Avila: "The Gospel is not a bag of lead which one drags around arduously, but a font of joy that fills the heart with God and impels it to serve one's brothers and sisters!" Our faith is a font of joy—this joy should overflow within us and permeate every day of our lives. Spreading the love of Christ is so much about spreading joy in all that we do. Does that mean you aren't supposed to feel sad emotions or ever be unhappy? No. Those are natural emotions and part of life. But life is too short to spend it taking everything really seriously and being the person who is complaining and bringing everyone down all the time.

Of course, there are some things that we must give up if we decide to follow Jesus. Those things certainly include sinful lifestyles and sinful ways. Jesus says there are things we have to leave behind if we are going to follow him, and he makes that very clear in his exchange with the rich young man in Matthew 19. But it is important to realize that our world needs people who love Jesus but who are completely assimilated into a normal, everyday life. There have been many saints and beatified young people who enjoyed and participated in the everyday life of the world around them. St. Philip Neri is known for his dazzling zest for living, humor, and practical jokes. Bl. Pier Giorgio Frassati was a young man who loved the outdoors, hiking, and mountain climbing, who often went on adventurous excursions with friends and incorporated his radical love for Christ into every facet of his life.

One of my favorite examples of a young woman who lived a holy life and enjoyed her life at the same time was Bl. Chiara Luce Badano. Chiara was born in Italy in 1971. She was dedicated to her faith at a very young age, and she attended high school like a regular young woman. She was a normal teenager—she listened to pop music, played sports, and loved the outdoors. She even struggled in school! Some of her peers teased her by calling her "Sister" because of her dedication to her faith. When Chiara was sixteen, she was diagnosed with a painful bone cancer. She suffered for two years with beautiful dignity and grace, constantly uniting her suffering with the suffering of Jesus—which paved the way to her beatification in the Catholic Church. Bl. Chiara is a beautiful example of the reality that you and I can be completely immersed in the normal, everyday world but live a holy and full dedication to Jesus—all at the same time.

In the twenty-first century, our call to evangelize looks like living in the world and shining the light of Christ into the places that really, really need it. You can play soccer, listen to music, go to concerts, and hang out with your friends, so long as you always maintain a discerning eye about things that may lead you away from God.

The things that we have talked about in this book are challenging, but they aren't meant to be like a ball and chain around your neck, preventing you from dancing, singing, or enjoying your life. Be goofy. Sing in the shower. Go camping. Sew clothes. Decorate your home. Grow a garden. Play ultimate frisbee. Throw random dance parties.

You can do all these things for God's glory. He wants you to be totally, completely, wholeheartedly you. You can incorporate all that we have talked about in this book and still be a completely modern, funny, engaging, positive, cheerful woman. The Christian life is not a life of doom and gloom, serious conversations, and being stuck in a chapel to pray twenty-four hours a day. The Christian life is one of intense joy, and it can provide immense opportunities for enjoying the magnificence of life and loving Christ all at the same time.

Don't be afraid to live. Take time to stop and smell the roses. Don't ever be afraid to enjoy your life. Keep your heart fixed on God, the artist responsible for all goodness and joy, and *just be you.*

. . . .

TAKE ACTION

Make a conscious effort to do something that you really love to do but seldom have time for. Make time for you, and enjoy it!

Conclusion

One of my favorite heroines of the Bible is Esther. She is a strong, bold woman in scripture who had to muster up great bravery to do what she knew God was calling her to do. In the book of Esther, she prays a powerful prayer to God, calling upon him to equip her with the bravery needed to approach the king in order to save her people. She prays: "Remember, O Lord; make yourself known in this time of our affliction, and *give me courage*, O King of the gods and Master of all dominion! . . . Save us by your hand, and *help me, who am alone and have no helper but you, O Lord*" (Esther 14:12, 14, emphasis added).

As we finish our journey here together, I thought it fitting to write a prayer of bravery for the modern-day woman, calling upon the Lord in the same way Esther did. I pray this prayer with you and for you in this moment, because you and I are in this together.

. . . .

Jesus, I love you with my whole heart. It is not always easy to follow you. It is not easy to be brave in carrying my light. There are days when I don't feel courageous or strong enough. Please be present to me in my times of struggle, and give me the grace to carry on forward and shine my light. I ask that you bring out the valiant spirit that you instilled within me at the moment you brought me into existence and tenderly created my soul. Help me to recognize that I am a woman of valor, honor, dignity, and grace. Lord, give me the courage to say no to the things that will pull me away from you. Grant me the bravery to say yes to the things that will lead me closer to you and to your heart. Give me the grace to see that you have given me permission to shine as the glorious woman I am. When I forget who I am, help me to get in tune with the song that heaven has always been singing over my life—the song you are always singing—the song of who I am and who you created me to be. Give me an indefatigable resolve to build your kingdom on earth. I want to be your hands and feet. I want to live out the unique and unrepeatable call you have designed for my life. Help me to recognize that it is not up to me to use my gifts—it is up to me to depend on you to help me use them. Give me the grace to be a humble vessel of your love, to love quietly in the moments where quiet love is needed and to love loudly when loud love is needed. I pray that my love may always be radical, that my love may always show the world that you are alive, living and breathing, your everlasting heartbeat inside of mine. Make me fearless in the face of adversity, courageous in the dark nights of loneliness, and inexhaustible when the temptations to quit arise in my heart. Help me to look to you to fulfill my aching desires for importance, for affirmation, for love. You see me. You know me. You love me. Jesus, help me to be radiant. Jesus, help me to go bravely.

Go bravely: all will be well, have no fear.

– ST. JOAN OF ARC

Acknowledgments

Thank you to my husband, Daniël. Your deep, unwavering strength and cheerfulness continually push me onward. Your love is a miracle I never saw coming—thank you for sharing in life with me. To my family—Dad, Mom, Anna May, John Paul, Gracie, Tommy, Aunt Janie, and baby Thomas—I love you all and thank you for your never-ending, continuous love and support of what God has called me to do. Dad, I have never once questioned if my father loves me, believes in me, or would do anything for me. Thank you for this incalculable gift. Mom, you are a graceful warrior who has shown us all how to live the "little way." I love you. Thank you to all the Wilsons, to Bernadette and my family in the Netherlands, my Life Teen family, and all the girls who I got to know in campus ministry. I am deeply grateful to my beloved mentor, Mrs. Nick—I miss you so, my dear friend. Thank you to every woman who has ever taught me how to live what I wrote in these pages by your example—you have shown me the way. To Kristi McDonald, my editor, thank you for your enthusiasm and support on the journey of writing this book.

And to every woman who has ever shared your heart with me, in person or online—your trust, your joy, and your vulnerability have changed everything. You are the reason this book exists. Thank you for lighting up my life.

Notes

TWO: REMEMBER WHO YOU ARE
John Paul II, apostolic letter *Mulieris Dignitatem: On the Dignity and Vocation of Women* (Boston: St. Paul Books and Media, 1988).

SEVEN: FIND YOUR GAGGLE
Library of Congress, "Why Do Geese Fly in a V?" Everyday Mysteries, accessed August 20, 2017, https://www.loc.gov/rr/scitech/mysteries/geese.html.

EIGHT: CHOOSE CHASTITY
Edith Stein, *Essays on Woman,* translated by Freda Mary Oben (Washington, DC: Institute of Carmelite Studies Publications, 1987).
Catechism of the Catholic Church (CCC).

FIFTEEN: KEEP CALM AND FOLLOW GOD
Edith Stein, *Essays on Woman,* translated by Freda Mary Oben (Washington, DC: Institute of Carmelite Studies Publications, 1987).

Benedict XVI, "Mass, Imposition of the Pallium, and Conferral of the Fisherman's Ring for the Beginning of the Petrine Ministry of the Bishop of Rome, Homily of His Holiness Benedict XVI," Vatican Website, accessed July 20, 2017, https://w2.vatican.va/content/benedict-xvi/en/homilies/2005/documents/hf_ben-xvi_hom_20050424_inizio-pontificato.html.

TWENTY: LIVE IT UP

Francis, "Message of Pope Francis to the Bishop of Avila on the Occasion of the Opening of the Teresian Jubilee Year," Vatican Website, accessed September 19, 2017, https://w2.vatican.va/content/francesco/en/messages/pont-messages/2014/documents/papa-francesco_20141015_messaggio-500-teresa-avila.html.

EMILY WILSON HUSSEM is an international Catholic speaker, author, and musician who travels full-time to share her faith at numerous women's conferences and with youth and young adults at events such as Life Teen and Steubenville conferences and at parishes, dioceses, and schools.

The author of *I Choose the Sky*, she earned a bachelor's degree in broadcast journalism from Arizona State University. Wilson Hussem lives in Southern California with her husband, Daniël.

http://emwilsonmusic.com
Facebook: @emilywilsonministries
Twitter, Instagram: @emwilss
Youtube: youtube.com/emilyywilsonn

AVE

AVE MARIA PRESS

Founded in 1865, Ave Maria Press, a ministry of the Congregation of Holy Cross, is a Catholic publishing company that serves the spiritual and formative needs of the Church and its schools, institutions, and ministers; Christian individuals and families; and others seeking spiritual nourishment.

———— ·◆· ————

For a complete listing of titles from

Ave Maria Press

Sorin Books

Forest of Peace

Christian Classics

visit www.avemariapress.com

AVE | AVE MARIA PRESS
     | Notre Dame, IN
A Ministry of the United States Province of Holy Cross